YOU CAN'T SERVE THEM WELL
IF YOU DON'T
KNOW THEM WELL:
Capturing and Captivating Customers
with
Concierge Customer Service™

Jeanne Hurlbert, PhD

and

Randy MacLean

Table of Contents

"I am struck by the fear that ultimately drives larger, mature businesses, and I contrast that with the fearlessness that is needed to create a new one. I'd love to be able to pinpoint that singular moment in a business's lifecycle when the culture changes from innovation to risk mitigation." – Marti Beller

CHAPTER 1: Capturing the Opportunity in Disruption with Customer-Centric Innovation

Things are tough for wholesale distributors these days—and they're getting tougher. The challenges of disintermediation, technological transformation, increased threat from traditional and nontraditional competitors, and the sheer pace of change have left many wholesale distributors struggling to stand as the ground shakes violently beneath them.

Does any of this sound like your company?
- You're feeling margin pressures,
- You're suffering under escalating personnel costs,
- You're watching your best customers defect to competitors whom you *know* aren't as good as your company is,
- You feel your business model isn't as relevant to the market as it was 10-20 years ago, or
- Your company lacks the flexibility or budget to do things it used to do.

If any of these things sound like what you're experiencing right now, you're not alone. In his book *Innovate*, Dirk Beveridge (2014, p. 4) cites results of a

National Association of Wholesaler-Distributors (NAW) survey of "C-suite" executives and vice presidents of member companies. The insights that emerged confirmed these executives' perceptions of the unique, disruptive environment in which they operate: "[Seventy-six percent] of distributors surveyed said they believe we are living in an environment we could call 'the age of disruption.'"

To survive in this disruptive environment, you *must* innovate, you *must* change, and you *must* do so in a *customer-centric* way. What does it mean to be customer-centric? It means understanding your customer's needs and ensuring that they're satisfied with the extent to which you meet those needs. To do so successfully, you *must* understand the true nature of the changing market in which you operate. Among the disruptive trends you face in the market are:

- Millennials (born between 1979 and 1994 (Smola and Sutton, 2002))—the largest birth cohort of the last century—now comprise the **largest** generational segment of the US workforce (US Bureau of the Census).

  Your company must increasingly adapt to the dictum that "Millennials are different." And the key to marketing to Millennials lies in understanding who they are and what "keeps them awake at night."

- One of the things that distinguishes Millennials is their level of trust. Although surveys show clearly that about 31% of "Generation X" members say most people can be trusted and 40% of "Baby Boomers" evince this trust, only 19% of Millennials express this level of trust (Drake, 2014).

You must increasingly work to earn the trust of your prospects and customers by showing them you understand, at a deep level, who they are and what their priorities are.

- Geography has become less of a barrier, creating a situation in which your prospects and customers can, and do, search online through hundreds of your competitors. And they know well that they can as easily purchase from competitors who lie thousands of miles away from you as they can purchase from you.

  You must increasingly provide an exceptional customer experience or risk losing your customers to competitors.

- Millennials and their older counterparts increasingly use new technologies to communicate, relying on devices and analytics (such as social media and online search), rather than print ads, to gather information.

  You can't expect your customers to adapt to your technology. You must adapt to theirs. To do so, you must understand how your customers prefer to communicate and order.

The kind of rapid industrial, technological, and social change you are facing demands radical solutions and fast action. But sometimes, those solutions don't have to be radically *new*, just radically *simple*. As simple as going back to the basics—the basics of generating profit by connecting with your customers. Because, after all, generating profit is *your* paramount responsibility.

Profit fuels growth. Profit enables you to provide better benefits to your employees. Profit facilitates charitable giving for your organization. And your ability to generate profit effectively boils down to your ability to **convert revenue to profit**. All kinds of conversions—of leads to customers, revenue to cash flow, cash flow to your bottom line, trucks on the road into deliveries—stand at the heart and soul of your business, determining how profitable you will be. And one of the best ways to generate profit in your company is to differentiate your company from your competitors. To do that, you must change radically the conception of customer service that has prevailed in wholesale distribution for decades.

Before we get into the specifics of what you can do to increase profit in the midst of this tumultuous change, let's look back to another time of great social upheaval. Doing so will allow us to identify underlying social dynamics that will help us understand and put into context the current transformation, so we appreciate *why* what is happening *is* happening.

The Opportunity of Change

Baron Rothschild, scion of the renowned banking family, gave the famously-macabre admonition to "buy when there is blood in the streets." Whether or not you view this as sound investment advice, the statement highlights the opportunity that times of great social change bring. Businesspeople who are savvy enough to avoid panic in times like these will reap the rewards of that opportunity.

I hold a PhD in sociology, a discipline that emerged in another time of rapid change and social upheaval. The

Industrial Revolution of the late 18th and 19th centuries transformed not just the way in which we produced goods but also the very fabric of society. A combination of "push" factors, including policies such as the Enclosure Acts, and "pull" factors like the emerging urban factory system fueled unprecedented rural-to-urban migration. Every aspect of social life—from family structure to education to political dynamics to religion—underwent fundamental challenge and change. Those who lived through that era became, for the first time in human history, acutely aware of social change. Why was that new? Because up until that point, the pace of social change in society had generally been so slow that most individuals remained largely unaware of it. Suddenly, then, society saw not just awareness of social change but also the need to adapt to it.

Given this profound social transformation—a transformation not unlike the disruptive environment we're experiencing right now—it's not surprising that a discipline whose focus is to understand, explain, and predict the nature of social change and social structure emerged. That discipline, sociology, was founded in part by a 19th-century German named Max Weber. Weber's work, particularly his organizational insights, proved so consequential that it continues to inform our understanding of social organization even today. Sociology, and specifically Weber's work, can help us understand and navigate the disruptive environment in which we are now required to operate.

One of the reasons that Weber's analysis has had such staying power is because he recognized the importance that *bureaucracy* would play in an increasingly-complex society. Although the term *bureaucracy* often carries negative connotations today, it actually denotes a way of organizing to get things done efficiently. Weber recognized that as societies, governments, and businesses reached increasing size and complexity, bureaucratic systems would be necessary to administer those organizations. Why? Because bureaucratic systems bring two key benefits: *specialization* and *division of labor*. The growth of bureaucracy was, for Weber, part and parcel of the increasing *rationalization* of society, in which social life increasingly depended not upon personal relationships but instead upon rational principles and systems of organization, and upon economic transactions (Weber 1978).

But Weber also recognized and described the "dark side" of bureaucracy and rationalization. Although he viewed bureaucracies as inevitable and recognized their advantages for achieving an organization's goals, he also warned that bureaucracy could become an *inefficient* "iron cage" that could frustrate both the individuals who worked within bureaucratic systems and the individuals—like your customers—who dealt with them. The very organization that could, and should, *increase* organizational efficiency and goal attainment could, in many cases, create *inefficiencies* that subverted their success.

Most wholesale distribution companies today, even those that remain family owned, are of sufficient size and scale to embody characteristics of bureaucracy. Yet there are many ways in which your companies may actually have *under leveraged* specialization and division of labor within your organization, missing the benefits that bureaucracy can bring. But rest assured . . . We can change this!

This book will show you how to free yourself from Weber's "iron cage" so that you can reap the benefits of *specialization* and *division of labor* while still enjoying an organizational culture that rewards your employees and benefits your customers. To understand how that's possible, let's start with some very simple concepts.

Where This All Began

Long before I earned a PhD or began working with wholesale distributors, I learned a lot about the power of connecting with customers growing up in a tiny town in rural North Carolina. My father, a country banker in the hamlet of Sunbury, saw business as a mission to *serve people well*. And he understood clearly that **you can't serve them well if you don't know them well**. That's why he used "business intelligence," long before either he or the customers he served had any clue what that term meant. The "business intelligence" that underlay his consistent success proved startlingly simple: Connect with your customers to understand *who they are* and *what they need*, then ensure that you give them what they need. And when a problem arises, fix it.

In that simple world, he could connect with his customers and understand their needs just by walking into the bank lobby and shaking hands with the customers he served. And he did that religiously, greeting the struggling farmer and the local physician with equal regard. They knew he cared about them and they knew he brought a true servant's heart to his role, whether that meant helping a farmer to build a house when no other bank would take a chance on him, providing the loan that would bring indoor plumbing to a struggling family, or helping a family save their farm when things got tough. I received this message a few years ago from a woman with whom I grew up, describing the impact my father's decisions had on the family:

I just returned from a very special trip to NC. My sister and I went to Nags Head and finally scattered the last of my Mom's ashes off Jeanette's Fishing Pier into the ocean she loved so much. We talked of many things, but one story that continued to pop up repeatedly was one of your father and how he helped my father secure our farm. He played a tremendous role, and I'm quite certain that it would never happen again quite like that. Had it not been for his trust and kindness, my Dad would have lost this farm we love so much and whose productivity continues to flourish.

If you think this means my father exercised free-wheeling loan policies that paved the way for the mortgage debacle, think again. He maintained one of the best loan ratios of any bank around. How? Because he knew the people, which meant he knew when it was wise to take a chance on someone and when the risk was simply too high.

The reality is that you can have a dramatic impact on your customers. Every business owner can, **if** you commit to knowing and serving your customers well. And one of the things we love about wholesale distribution companies is that most of you genuinely strive to serve your customers well. The key to doing so, while still remaining profitable, lies in doing exactly what my father did: Gathering the intelligence you need to understand who your customers are and what they need, then using that intelligence to serve your customers at the highest level. Although most of you can't gather intelligence with personal handshakes the way my father did, we're going to show you how you can use modern, scientific methods to gather the same kind of information and use it to serve your customers. This will differentiate your company in the marketplace simply because these fundamentals of business aren't being executed by your competitors.

The Erosion of Service

The world we just described has largely ceased to exist—not only because of technology or urbanization or the pace of social change, but also because the *art and science of customer service* have become increasingly rare in American commerce. Any one of us can recount stories of poor—sometimes outrageously poor—customer service that not only left us frustrated but also engendered resentment toward the company that appeared to care so little about the customers who generate its profits.

Let's review a recent example of bad service. I dealt with a cable company whose name, ironically, included the word "communications." Technician after technician had come to repair my internet service, but horrendous problems persisted. When I recently made yet another call to customer service, I navigated an automated menu and then spent 10 minutes on hold before I spoke with a customer service representative about the ongoing problems. Because the problems had been so persistent, the customer service agent relayed me to the "customer loyalty" department, assuring me that they would have all the details of my problems and would be empowered to solve them. But when I reached that department, they knew nothing about the issues, had no authority to solve my problems, and simply sent me back to the automated menu, where I waited for another 15 minutes before speaking with a second customer service representative.

That representative seemed sympathetic to the problem and assured me that she knew just the office that could help. She not only transferred me to that office but also gave her their direct number, in case I was disconnected and needed to call back. But my hopes were dashed when I discovered that this department was for internal use only and, without an access code, I could not reach anyone in it. So back to the automated menu I went.

By the time I reached the third customer service representative, this process had consumed 45 minutes of my busy morning. The only remedy that the third representative could offer was to send yet another technician to attempt to solve the problem. By this point, I stood ready to move quickly to one of the company's competitors. Soon after, I cancelled my account.

Here lies an excellent illustration of the "iron cage," of systems created to solve problems that end up undermining the company's goals and alienating its customers. Unfortunately, this story proves all too familiar in both business-to-consumer and business-to-business markets. The consequences of experiences like this can prove staggering for your business. Consider these facts:

- A survey by Dimensional Research (2013) found that customer service affects people's trust in vendors;

- That same survey found that nearly 2/3—62%—of business-to-business (B2B) customers purchased more after a *positive* experience with customer service, but 66% *ceased buying* if that customer service experience was bad; and
- In B2B markets, 51% avoided vendors as much as two years after a bad customer service experience (Dimensional Research, 2013).

If these effects aren't sufficient to motivate you to "up the game" on your customer service, just remember that your customers no longer feel consigned to suffer in silence. Online reviews affect not only decisions in the business-to-consumer (B2C) but also in the B2B space. For instance:

- A recent study by Deloitte reveals that 1 in 4 (25%) of all Americans do "comparison shopping" on the web (Keckley and Coughlin, 2012).
- Fully 74%—nearly 3 in 4—of surveyed respondents say that positive reviews increase their trust in a local business (BrightLocal, 2016).
- A 2016 study by BrightLocal (2016) revealed that 84% of consumers trust online reviews as much as personal recommendations.
- Harvard Business Review published results of a sophisticated analysis[1] showing that a one-star increase in Yelp ratings produced a 5-9% increase in revenue for restaurants (Luca, 2016).

---

[1] The analysis used multiple regression to estimate the net effect of a rating increase on restaurant revenue.

- Healthcare consumers are becoming just as savvy as their counterparts in other sectors: A survey by Price-Waterhouse Cooper's Health Research Institute showed that nearly half (48%) of consumers had read healthcare reviews online; of those, more than 2/3—68%—of respondents said those reviews affected their healthcare choices (Healthcare Research Institute, 2013).
- Even churches are being reviewed on such sites as Yelp and Churchrater.com.

Online reviews give you yet another reason to ensure that you serve your customers well—because good news and bad news can spread with equal speed.

Your Concierge Customer Service Edge

In this age of uncertainty, one thing remains certain: Things are as tough and confusing for your customers as they are for you. Like you, they're looking for an edge. They're looking for a way to make things easier, to cut through the clutter to do their jobs and stay in business and maybe even eke out a profit.

That's where your opportunity lies: You can give your best customers the edge they're looking for and improve *your* profits in the process. **Concierge Customer Service (CCS)** achieves that goal by giving your most profitable customers a level of service that not only makes their lives and jobs easier but also improves the customers' efficiency. That's why CCS proves to be such a win-win for your company: Because the CCS system provides your top customers with such profit-generating perks as fast and efficient problem resolution, priority call on inventory availability, and preferred pricing, the benefits of the system flow to your customers' bottom lines *and* to yours. Your company can differentiate itself in the marketplace by making a new, compelling case for doing business with you, creating a marketplace bias toward your company that inheres not in the friendly smiles of your donut-delivering sales force, but in the increased efficiency and profitability of your customers.

You begin to see, then, why and how Concierge Customer Service can drive growth in your company. The myriad benefits of this system include, but are not limited to, **Conversion, Penetration of your market, and Retention—CPR.**

Conversion benefits derive when you draw from your competitors the customers who resemble closely your most profitable customers. Why can you do that? Because this exceptional level of service, a level your competitors cannot afford to match, becomes a potent tool for your sales team, who can now offer solid, *rational* reasons for doing business with you.

Penetration of your market increases as the benefits of your Concierge Customer Service system become apparent to other customers—in particular your marginal accounts. Once those accounts see the advantages your top-tier customers gain, the marginal accounts will want access to those benefits. That gives you the opportunity to show less profitable customers what actions to take to secure the higher-level service. *Those actions, of course, are the actions that will make those accounts profitable for you.*

Retention benefits emerge particularly among your most profitable customers, who are the **only** customers who receive true **Concierge Customer Service.** You achieve those benefits in three ways:

1. You provide your most profitable customers with a level of service that your competitors *can't*, making it impossible for those competitors to steal your most profitable customers away from you. The retention benefits will actually extend beyond your top-tier customers: Because the mindset of Concierge Customer Service will "trickle down" through your organization to change its very culture, and because this system will provide feedback from customers at *all* levels of profitability, you will glean retention benefits across the board. That means you can retain more of the customers whom you *want* to keep.

2. Second, by implementing the Concierge Customer Service system, you ensure exceptional levels of customer satisfaction and loyalty throughout your organization because you constantly garner customer input through the Feedback Generator.

3. Third, this system will increase the frequency and the quality of communication between your operating team and your customers' operating teams, building rapport, increasing loyalty, and engendering a feeling of true partnership between you and your customer.

In addition to these CPR benefits, your Concierge Customer Service system can increase your profitability through these additional mechanisms:

1. **Increased flow of leads**—The Concierge Customer Service system's Feedback Generator produces a constant flow of testimonials, satisfaction data, referrals, and even online reviews with virtually no effort, dramatically increasing your ability to attract qualified prospects. That's how you simply and easily benefit from specialization and division of labor in lead generation and conversion.

2. **Continuous process improvement**—The statistical satisfaction data from your Feedback Generator not only demonstrate how satisfied your customers are, overall, but also identify specific areas in which you enjoy opportunities for improvement, in your customer service and beyond. For example, the overall statistical data may show you that 95% of your customers are satisfied but the specific data may still show that they're less satisfied with your website than they are with other areas. That pattern shows you *exactly* where you need to improve. By gathering clear, concise information from your customers, you can address areas that need your attention and look for ways to increase your customers' positive experiences doing business with you.

3. **Customer service bellwethers**—If a customer proves to be dissatisfied, the Feedback Generator should alert your customer service team so that they can respond quickly. If that disgruntled customer is a CCS customer, a dedicated representative will solve the problem. If the customer is not in the top tier, other representatives can contact the customer to

understand and resolve the issue. This rapid response system allows you to identify and resolve issues *before* they cost you customers and dollars.

4. ***Personnel benefits*—**Because they show you *exactly* where problems lie, the data that your Feedback Generator provide show you how to reduce not only customer service complaints, but also issues related to ordering, deliverability, accounting, and invoicing. As you solve those problems and reduce complaints, your customer service personnel will hear from far fewer irritated customers and spend more of their time building relationships with customers and less time solving problems. That, in turn, will increase the representatives' job satisfaction.

But what of the other customers, those who don't qualify for this exceptional level of service? The Concierge Customer Service system ensures that these customers will always receive a high level of service—just not the exceptional level offered to their more-profitable counterparts.

By coupling the institution of Concierge Customer Service with intentional use of specialization and division of labor—especially between your sales and customer service teams—the gains for your customers, your company, your personnel, and your profits can prove great.

Steps to Becoming Customer-Centric
Implementing Concierge Customer Service can be accomplished with three simple steps:

1. In Phase I, you answer the two most important, but frequently unanswered questions in business: (a) "what do your customers *want*?" and (b) "how satisfied are they with the extent to which you are *giving them what they want*?"
2. In Phase II, you leverage the answers to those questions to customize your Concierge Customer Service system for your business, so that you offer high-level customer service to all of your customers and Concierge Customer Service to your most profitable customers, and then
3. In Phase III, you maintain a high-caliber *system* to measure customer sentiment, consistently and effectively, to ensure you constantly (a) serve your customers well by knowing them well and (b) fuel your marketing with testimonials and statistical data that most of your competitors lack.

After providing you with more detail on the 4 pillars of Concierge Customer Service, we walk you through each of the phases of Concierge Customer Service, showing you exactly how to put your system in place and use it effectively.

Figure 1.1

Where We're Going

CHAPTER 1	CHAPTER 2	CHAPTER 3	CHAPTER 4
How to Identify and Capture Your Opportunity	The Keys to Becoming Customer-Centric	Why You Can Afford It	Phase I: Knowing Them Well

CHAPTER 8	CHAPTER 7	CHAPTER 6	CHAPTER 5
Your Action Items	Different Strokes for Different (Generational) Folks	Phase III: Ensuring You Keep Knowing and Serving Them Well	Phase II: Serving Them Well

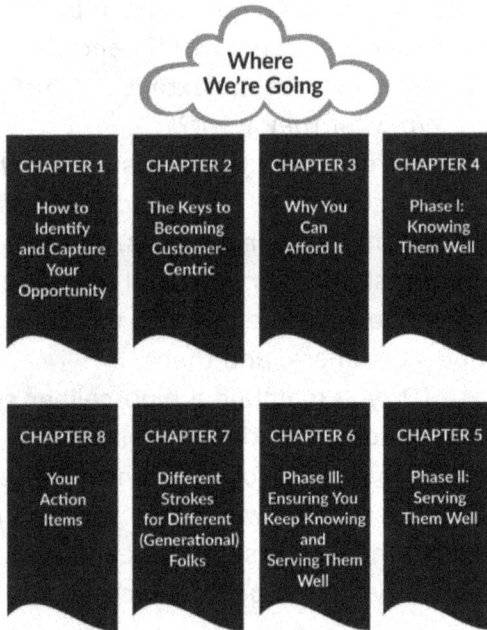

Rescuing Your Customers from the Iron Cage

The facts remain clear: Your customers seek an *experience* with you. Dan Sullivan, founder of The Strategic Coach, has said that "[t]he only way to create value is in someone else's future." Your opportunity lies in crafting the experience your customers crave, to create value in their futures. Both of you can escape the "iron cage" of bureaucracy if you capitalize on the structural benefits of bureaucracy at the same time you infuse life into your company. Beth Comstock, Vice Chair of General Electric, describes innovation in their company as an endeavor to "think like a venture capital company." She articulates two core missions in GE:

1. Take care of customers
2. Grow and Innovate

We encourage you to embrace these same two missions in your company by implementing Concierge Customer Service, using the steps we outline.

Conclusion

As you can see, the combination of societal pressures mired in an ever-changing consumer dynamic can produce a minefield that wholesale distribution companies like yours must navigate. By instituting a system to measure, interpret, and refine customer engagement and experience, your business can be poised to maximize your advantages while mitigating risks from your markets. So let's get started.

"Whether you are big or small, you cannot give good customer service if your employees don't feel good about coming to work." – Martin Oliver

CHAPTER 2: Giving Customers MORE: The Four Pillars of Concierge Customer Service

Now you see your opportunity: To retain your best, most profitable customers by providing Concierge Customer Service to them and, in so doing, capture more customers *like* them. Doing so allows you to capitalize upon two of the key benefits of bureaucracy—*specialization* and *division of labor*—while avoiding the bureaucratic inefficiencies that can conspire to create an "iron cage" for both your customers and your employees. ***This is how you reap the benefits of specialization and division of labor while enjoying an organizational culture that rewards your employees and benefits your customers.***

Remember . . . we are focusing on your customers *and* your employees—because, as we establish below, keeping your *customers* satisfied requires that you also keep your *employees* satisfied. In other words, being "customer-centric"—becoming a company whose mission focuses squarely on the customers who generate your profit—means that you must simultaneously be "employee-centric." As Ken Blanchard and Colleen Barrett describe in their book *Lead with LUV*, Southwest Airlines embodies this principle. Because Southwest is so famously customer-centric, one might expect that their idea of "leading with LUV" would be to put their customers first. But they explain that they actually put their *employees* first; their customers come second, followed by their shareholders. As Blanchard puts it, "[s]ervant leaders know that financial success is a byproduct of how their people and their customers are treated" (Blanchard and Barrett, 2010). So in this chapter, we not only outline the core elements of Concierge Customer Service but also detail how to factor your employees into the equation.

Becoming Customer-Centric

One of the byproducts of the increase in customer-centric companies has been the expansion of the Chief Customer Officer. In 2003, fewer than twenty companies in the world employed a Chief Customer Officer (CCO), but by 2015 more than 1 in 10 Fortune 500 companies and over 1 in 5 Fortune 100 companies had instituted that role. What does a Chief Customer Officer do? He or she:

- Ensures that the company understands who their customers or clients are, at a deep level;
- Builds lasting relationships with those customers; and
- Ensures that they serve those customers at the highest level.

Despite the increasing recognition of the *importance* of becoming customer-centric, research suggests that many companies fall short in their ability to actually *be* customer-centric. A 2014 survey of senior marketing executives showed that, although 73% of respondents viewed customer-centric focus as critical to their success and that of their organizations, only 14% said that customer-centricity could be considered a "hallmark" of their companies and only 11% thought their customers would characterize their companies as customer centric. ***Those statistics suggest that many companies pay only "lip service" to being customer centric.***

Once again, your opportunity emerges from the shortcomings of your competitors. ***To compete successfully in today's environment, you must commit to becoming customer centric by putting in place the systems that ensure you will actually be customer centric.*** Designating a CCO increases the probability that Concierge Customer Service will achieve the desired results. Why? Because Concierge Customer Service has the highest probability of success when it is led by someone for whom the customer is their *chief* priority, rather than just *one* of their priorities. That's why your company must seriously consider how you prioritize this key strategy. For example, if you operate a relatively small business with limited personnel, you may not be able to devote a full-time staff member to serve as a CCO. In that case, consider putting your best people-facing manager in place and make the responsibility for Concierge Customer Service half of his or her role.

Establishing a Chief Customer Officer dovetails beautifully with another critically-important trend, the creation of the ***Chief Profit Officer (CPO)***. The CPO:

- Elevates the importance of profitability,
- Evaluates the profitability of various actions,
- Ensures the company pursues profitable strategies, and also
- Ensures that customer service remains paramount in priorities and practices.

Establishing these two C-Level roles ensures that the intertwined outcomes of profitability and customer service receive the priority they deserve. Instituting them formally differentiates your company in the marketplace and does much to ensure your success.

Understanding the Elements of Concierge Customer Service

The objective in establishing Concierge Customer Service is to deliver a differentiated, distinct, exceptional customer experience to your most profitable customers—and really *good* service to all customers—by giving customers MORE: **mindset, ownership, referability**, and **experience**. It means giving your customers *more* than your competitors give and often *more* than your customers expect. To maximize the conversion, penetration, and retention benefits of Concierge Customer Service, giving customers MORE should be come more than just policy—it must become part of your culture, something ingrained in your corporate DNA. Achieving that doesn't require anything mysterious or magical. It's primarily about executing the fundamentals, executing them well, and executing them consistently.

Let's look more closely at what this really means. Certainly most companies have a customer service department, but in wholesale distribution, the term "customer service" has become a code word for "order entry." Because customer service representatives receive the orders, they're also the people who talk to customers and are tasked with resolving customer problems and complaints. You may call that customer service, but that's not Concierge Customer Service. ***Concierge Customer Service requires MORE—a reality in which customer service means not just expedient ordering but also reliable problem resolution.***

Concierge Customer Service is, by definition, EXTRAordinary, going "above and beyond" what is typical. In a 5-star hotel, you might receive such amenities as having your bags transported for you, being greeted throughout the hotel by your name at all times, and enjoying complimentary limousine service. The level of service that your most profitable customers receive should feel just as frictionless and extraordinary. Let's look at the 4 key elements of Concierge Customer Service, the components of giving your customers MORE.

The Concierge Customer Service Mindset

Mindset means that the people who own customer service in your organization need to be:

- Good listeners
- Patient
- Oriented towards solving problems rather than providing excuses
- Lifelong learners who embody a *growth mindset* rather than a *fixed mindset*, people who *want* to learn new things and *learn how to put them into action*.

This also requires that you, as the business leader, support CCS representatives in that learning process by providing, supporting, and rewarding learning and growth opportunities.

The Concierge Customer Service mindset entails being able to "take the role of other" easily and often, which means Concierge Customer Service representatives know how to gather details on a problem and find out what the *customer* wants. Their ability to understand well the customer's point of view, taking notes to ensure that they do so, will prove critical to customer satisfaction, loyalty, and retention—and when you supplement it with a birds-eye view of customer preferences, through the **Opportunity Generator,** you increase both retention of customers and conversion of prospects. These individuals must embody the concept of a *servant's heart*, which entails listening deeply to customers to understand who they are and what they need, so that they truly understand how to serve your customers.

Given these specific requirements and expectations, screening and hiring carefully becomes imperative. Assessments, such as the Kolbe A™ (which measures how individuals naturally take action) or the DiSC® profile can prove extremely useful. We highly recommend using detailed profiles interpreted by an experienced profiler to identify Customer Service Representatives (CSRs) and Concierge Customer Service Representatives (CCSRs) who will bring the right mindset to the positions.

Taking Ownership of Customer Outcomes

Ownership means that those charged with Concierge Customer Service take ownership of customers' problems, become advocates for the customer, and provide solutions, ensuring that they keep the customer apprised of each step through the process. One of the places in which we find many wholesale distribution companies falling short, in the eyes of their customers, is in their ability to advocate for customers when a problem arises. For your *representatives* to advocate successfully for the customer, *you* must fully support the CSR or CCSR within your organization, ensuring that she or he possesses the authority to solve problems and has clear avenues through which to get things done. That may mean that a CCSR can go directly to the warehouse to have something picked or that they can request a manager deliver what the customer needs.

As a mom I enjoyed a wonderful example of a company taking ownership of a problem: I ordered an item for my daughter, whose French class was taking a trip from south Louisiana to Canada—in the winter. One of the items I ordered was a sweater; but when the package arrived, I received not the wool sweater I had ordered but a lightweight cotton jacket that was no match for a Quebec winter. When I called the vendor, the customer service representative spent 30 minutes working to find the right substitute. Then she provided a 30% discount coupon and expedited shipping for the replacement item.

Becoming Referable

Imagine how motivated I was to tell other moms about this company, after that experience. This provides a wonderful example of how **referability** should follow automatically if the Concierge Customer Service process works well. When you provide an extraordinary experience, people will be ready, willing, and able to go generate new customers for you. This is true for two reasons. First, the "norm of reciprocity," a fundamental principle of social life, demonstrates that when you give something to someone, they're highly motivated to give you something in return. Second, when we find something exemplary—whether it's a wonderful new restaurant or a business that provides extraordinary customer service—we're immediately motivated to tell others about it. That's why Concierge Customer Service makes you so referable. ***Those referrals are gold for your business because they let you reach deep into your target market at exceedingly low cost and practically clone your best customers.***

Why is that the case? Because of a network principle called *homophily*. Simply put, the *homophily principle* means that we tend to be connected to others who are like us. So if one of your best, most profitable customers refers you to someone they know, the chances are good that the referral resembles closely the customer who generated the referral. The fundamental question you must ask yourself is: "Will your customers refer you or will they send others to your competitors?" The answer to that question is the ultimate measure of **customer loyalty**.

Ensuring the Experience

Providing an experience can be as simple as consistently executing the fundamentals—something many of your competitors probably fail to do. The Four Seasons Hotel seeks to "[s]ystematize the predictable so that [they] can humanize everything else." When you systematize predictable elements, you gain the ability to go "above and beyond" what is generally expected to provide that extraordinary experience. Continuing to provide a wonderful customer experience proves key to distinguishing your business in the marketplace. It is the key to referability, satisfaction, loyalty, and retention.

Providing a *meaningful* experience to your customers means you must first understand what's meaningful to *them*. What are their drivers? Are they focused on quality? Cost? Speed of delivery? Accuracy? Or must a meaningful experience embody all of these elements? To provide an experience that will delight your customers, you must first answer these questions. And we show you exactly how to do that in Chapter 4.

When you select, train, and motivate your Concierge Customer Service representatives so that they embody the 4 elements of Concierge Customer Service, you differentiate your business immediately. Just think of the number of times you've experienced some kind of problem and had a customer service agent shuffle the problem off to another agent—or worse, try to foist the problem back on you. When your Concierge Customer Service representatives respond to *any* problem by saying, "I'm so sorry this happened to you. I'm on it. Go back to your job, I'm going to take care of all of it, and I'm going to call you in a couple of hours and tell you how to solve your problem or I'll tell you what's going on," you change the game in your business. The key to your success lies in finding people who will make that happen because they have the right *Mindset*, they take *Ownership* consistently, they provide an exceptional *Experience*, and they make you imminently *Referable*. Then, make sure your employees implement the system as you intend, by ensuring *their* satisfaction, as well.

The Link Between Employee Attitudes and Customer Satisfaction

Southwest's recognition of the vital link between employee and customer attitudes is supported by a large body of research—and this research shows the benefits can flow all the way to your bottom line. As Harvard Business Review reports, "companies with highly engaged people outperform firms with the most disengaged folks—by 54% in employee retention, by 89% in customer satisfaction, and by fourfold in revenue growth" (Goffee and Jones, 2013). Similarly, in a meta-analysis of 263 research studies conducted across 192 organizations in 49 industries, Gallup researchers underscored the connection between employee engagement and productivity: Work units in the top quartile in employee engagement outperformed bottom-quartile units by 10% on customer ratings, 22% in profitability, and 21% in productivity. Work units in the top quartile also saw significantly less turnover (25% in high-turnover organizations and 65% in low-turnover organizations), shrinkage (28%) and absenteeism (37%), and fewer safety incidents (48%), patient safety incidents (41%), and quality defects (41%; Reilly, 2013).

In an effort to assess whether employee attitudes actually increase customer satisfaction and productivity, rather than the reverse, British researchers used longitudinal data (i.e., data collected in the same organization over time) and found that employee commitment predicts both customer satisfaction and financial performance of the organization.

Job satisfaction also proves to be related to customer satisfaction. Based upon a meta-analysis documenting a positive relationship between employees' job satisfaction and customer satisfaction, researchers advise managers to "take actions that are likely to increase the job satisfaction of customer contact personnel" (Mendoza, and Maldonado, 2014). Another analysis, which used multiple studies spanning 7,939 business units in 36 companies, showed that employee satisfaction and engagement, at the business unit level, were related to outcomes in the business unit. This led the researchers to conclude that "changes in management practices that increase employee satisfaction may increase business-unit outcomes, including profit" (Harter, Schmidt, & Hayes, 2002). This is the reason that Southwest Airlines puts its people first, arguing that "internal customer service" (how employees treat each other, within your organization) and "external" customer service—to your customers—should become indistinguishable. Southwest established an "internal customer service team" to track employee birthdays, work anniversaries, and the like. Southwest sends cards to those employees, to the tune of over 100,000 cards per year.

Clearly, then, you have a vested interest in ensuring that your employees remain satisfied and engaged, as this can improve both your customers' satisfaction and your bottom line. As we outline in Chapter 4, doing so necessitates that you use well-designed surveys to measure employee attitudes at the beginning of your Concierge Customer Service journey. It also requires you to broaden your notions of what constitutes job satisfaction. Start by recognizing that you can't ensure your employees' satisfaction by meeting a fixed set of needs. Indeed, a voluminous literature has established that workers' job satisfaction depends in large part upon whether the characteristics a worker *values* in a job are *present* in the job.

Indeed, the idea that everyone's needs are the same has become outdated. Models that viewed job satisfaction in terms of meeting a hierarchy of fixed needs have been supplanted by models that recognize job satisfaction as dependent upon meeting workers' values and wants. Given that Maslow's theory positing a "hierarchy" of needs was first published in 1943, it shouldn't surprise us that new, more powerful models have emerged. These newer models recognize that workers' values and wants vary from employee to employee: Some workers might value pay over opportunities for self-expression, while others will sacrifice salary for growth opportunities and strong coworker relationships. ***That's why it is imperative to measure the extent to which employees perceive their jobs provide what they value.*** As your workforce increasingly includes Millennials, understanding what they value and measuring the extent to which they perceive they're getting what they value will become increasingly important.[2]

It is also important to understand that connections *among* your employees play a vital role in determining their job satisfaction. As an academic, I conducted research that shows your employees' job satisfaction is affected by the degree to which they connect to each other—the degree to which ties to coworkers show up in your employees' *social networks* (Hurlbert, 1991). When I use the term social

---

[2] In Chapter 7, we provide in-depth information on how Millennials, Generation X, and Baby Boomers differ.

network, I'm not talking just about their Facebook and LinkedIn connections—social media. We all had social networks long before those enterprises began and social scientists studied social networks decades before Mark Zuckerberg, Facebook's founder, was born. A social network includes anyone to whom an individual is connected, in any capacity. It encompasses friends, relatives, coworkers, neighbors, and anyone else with whom you have a relationship. Social networks vary in the extent to which they are comprised of these different types of individuals. Some people maintain primarily *strong ties* to close friends and relatives, while others have networks comprised almost exclusively of *weak ties* to friends-of-friends, acquaintances, and business connections.

The greater the extent to which your employees count their coworkers among their meaningful social connections, the more likely your employees are to be satisfied. Why? Because these social connections typically bring with them *social support*. The support might take the form of help solving a job-related problem (instrumental support) or emotional support that helps your employees cope with personal challenges outside the workplace.[3] That's why you have a vested interest in ensuring that connections among coworkers become, and remain, as numerous and healthy as possible.

---

[3] My academic research shows that the effects of that support can be dramatic: Data that my colleagues and I collected before and after Hurricane Katrina, under a grant from the National Science Foundation, showed that individuals whose social networks were better equipped to provide social support suffered lower rates of depression than those whose social networks were less robust.

Investing in your employees' engagement and satisfaction, then, means attending to the extent to which the characteristics they value in their jobs are present and also supporting meaningful coworker relationships. Being "employee-centric" in this way is one of the first step to becoming truly customer-centric.

Conclusion

Now that you understand how and why to implement Concierge Customer Service, we'll dig into the actual process, in the next three chapters. The first step to implementing Concierge Customer Service is to understand, through quantitative data, your employees' and customers' priorities and satisfaction (Chapter 4), then use that information to customize and implement your Concierge Customer Service system (Chapter 5). But first, we use the next chapter to provide detail on the financial foundations of Concierge Customer Service.

"The purpose of business is to create a customer who creates customers." – Shiv Singh

CHAPTER 3: How You Can Afford to Offer Service That Your Competitors Cannot

Because Concierge Customer Service is so extensive, it is an investment. That's why funding this service requires that you offer it only to the customers who generate the most profit for your business. In the wholesale distribution industry, roughly 30% of the customers generate nearly *all* of the profit in that business; about 20% of the customers generate losses large enough to wipe out 73% of the profits generated by the profitable customers. These numbers illustrate why Concierge Customer Service will likely extend only to the top 10-15% of your customers—the ones who transform revenue to profit at the highest rate.

How can you *identify* these highly-profitable customers? Through profit analytics, using WayPoint Analytics. WayPoint Analytics is a sophisticated profit and costing system used by distribution companies to identify unseen profit leaks and opportunities. Through WayPoint, you can focus your sales activities, optimize resource allocation, and free up cash flow. The system has been instrumental in identifying customer groups for Concierge Customer Service, new account targeting, ultra-competitive pricing, and record growth and profit rates.[4] Let's drill down into why it's so important to use a system like WayPoint to

---

[4] Find out more at www.waypointanalytics.net.

know to whom you can afford to deliver Concierge Customer Service.

The Financial Foundation of Concierge Customer Service

To further dissect the Concierge Customer Service model, consider again the example of 5-star hotels. These hotels cater to well-heeled clients who will pay handsomely for a room and for the amenities that the property offers. In exchange, the hotel offers them an exclusive level of treatment that is funded fully by the high profits that the room and amenity rates generate. Conceptually, *this should serve as the model by which your business differentiates or "tiers" its customer service, so that you offer good service to all customers but exceptional service only to the "top tier," whether you call them "Tier 1," "Platinum," or "A-List" customers.*

To remind you of *why* you differentiate your service levels in this way, consider again the benefits that we identified in Chapter 1. **Penetration of your market** increases as the benefits of your Concierge Customer Service system become apparent to other customers—in particular your marginal accounts. As those accounts see the advantages your top-tier customers gain and want access to those benefits, your salespeople can show these customers what actions to take to secure the higher-level service. *That provides a mechanism to transform money-losing into money-making accounts.* To achieve this gain, though, you must ensure that your salespeople understand the system, and the eligibility criteria, thoroughly. That's why Chapters 4 and 5 emphasize the importance of ensuring that your employees understand and support the system.

Retention benefits emerge particularly among your most profitable customers, who are the **only** customers who receive true **Concierge Customer Service.** To recap from Chapter 1, you achieve those benefits in three ways:

1. You provide your most profitable customers with a level of service that your competitors *can't*, making it impossible for those competitors to steal your most profitable customers away from you. And, as Concierge Customer Service takes root to transform the culture of your company, retention rates among less-profitable customers should also increase. That means you can retain more of the customers whom you *want* to keep, because you have rescued your customers from the "iron cage" of your competitors' bureaucracies.

2. As this cultural transformation takes place, you ensure exceptional levels of customer satisfaction and loyalty throughout your organization because you constantly garner customer input through the Feedback Generator. By gathering information most of your competitors lack, you keep your finger firmly on the pulse of customer sentiment, ensuring continuous process improvement.

3. As the frequency and the quality of communication between your operating team and your customers' operating teams increases, not only will you increase rapport and loyalty but you will also identify opportunities to increase sales to these existing customers.

We introduced the logic of identifying the Concierge Customer Service candidates—through profit segmentation—in the last chapter. **Your WayPoint profitability rankings will show you which customers are sufficiently profitable to fund Concierge Customer Service.** When you examine the Net Before Compensation (NBC)[5] ranking report or any profitability rankings in WayPoint, you will see something your competitors can't: The accounts with the highest volume are *not* necessarily the most profitable. Why? Because their cost-to-serve stands higher than that of many lower-volume accounts. Once WayPoint reveals those high-profit accounts, you can retain them and the profit they generate by providing them with service that far exceeds that of your competitors.

The **first thing to analyze** is the balance between operating cash and cost-to-serve dollars on every invoice, on every account, in every territory. **The math is simple: The profitability of your business depends upon whether the operating cash that you generate exceeds the cost-to-serve dollars consumed.** When you apply this principle to customer service, you recognize quickly the importance of watching this element carefully. Otherwise, you risk generating significant account attrition as you start to develop new priorities, processes, and systems. **You must retain the operating cash generation from your most profitable accounts.** Concierge Customer Service provides the mechanism for

---

[5] Net Before Compensation (NBC) shows the profit of a territory or customer after paying for the product and the infrastructure required to deliver the product to the customer. Its value lies in the fact that it eliminates the usual analytical distortions of sales compensation, thereby providing a clear picture of account or territory profitability.

doing so because it provides a mechanism for retaining those customers. This is the first benefit of CCS: Concierge Customer Service helps you manage the profits that come from your most profitable accounts, as we detail in Chapter 5, so that you maintain profitability on your top accounts.

For example, one of our clients found that, when they began offering Concierge Customer Service to 30 of their most profitable customers, they not only increased the retention rate in their top accounts but also created additional sales in all of those accounts, as the customer service representatives deepened the connection with and knowledge of those top accounts. They were also able to decrease the cost to serve of many less-profitable accounts: Because they discovered that many of these smaller customers wanted to order online, the company developed a campaign to ensure that these less-profitable customers understood clearly the benefits of online ordering and the steps to placing those orders.

Once you've assessed carefully the balance between operating cash and cost-to-serve dollars, the **second element** is to prepare for the eventual loss of operating cash from accounts that are actually losing money—that is, accounts in which the cost-to-serve dollars exceed the operating cash they create. The answer isn't to just "fire" these accounts immediately. Doing so would prove imprudent because you would have to either rationalize your infrastructure and personnel to compensate for the loss in operating cash, or garner additional operating cash to replace the operating cash lost from the "drain" accounts. That's why *your second step is to make the necessary*

***preparations to lose those accounts without hurting
your bottom line.***

That entails creating additional operating cash. How?
By attracting more customers who will be highly profitable.

To do that, you must identify companies who can
generate high levels of profit and then convert them. You
identify these potentially-profitable prospects by creating a
list of companies who resemble closely your top accounts—
often those who compete directly with them—and then
giving that list to your salespeople. Your salespeople can
convert them by offering them a service advantage—
Concierge Customer Service. You can *afford* to do so
because, as long as your logistics costs remain far below
the operating cash you generate, you can afford to earn
lower profit margins to woo those accounts away from your
competitors. Concierge Customer Service, then, quickly
becomes a wonderful **conversion tool** for attracting new
high-end customers. The more visible your Concierge
Customer Service engine becomes, the more powerfully it
draws those highly-profitable customers away from your
competitors.

Another factor that helps you achieve these
conversion benefits is mastering and managing cost-to-
serve and pricing. Here's a secret that many of your
competitors don't know: Our research shows that most
companies can offer 8-10% price (or margin) reduction to
your best accounts without losing money. In other words,
your most profitable accounts will likely remain profitable if
you reduce the margin by 8-10 points *without* impacting
your bottom line, as long as you give up some of your
money-losing accounts. Although we aren't suggesting that

you immediately approach your best customers and reduce prices, you *can* find customers that resemble closely your most profitable accounts or companies that generate 10-15% bottom line, net, on what they're bringing to you. If you reduce your margin by 1-2 points to bring in accounts that resemble closely these highly-profitable companies, you can have them give you 10%, rather than 15%, NBC (Net Before Compensation). In this way, you use the superior customer service strategies and pricing to go after your competitors' best accounts without affecting your bottom line, **thus increasing the conversion of companies who resemble closely your most profitable accounts.**

The Link to Sales Specialization and Division of Labor

In the companies with whom we work, the shift to the Concierge Customer Service system goes hand-in-hand with increased specialization of sales. In Chapter 1, we noted that two of the hallmarks of bureaucratic organization—two of the characteristics that make bureaucracies efficient—are *specialization* and *division of labor.* But in most wholesale distribution companies, the sales role continues to evidence a low level of specialization: Salespeople find themselves generating prospects, qualifying leads, setting appointments, making presentations, doing follow-up calls, providing customer service, and sometimes even bearing responsibility for account collections. That diverse sales role proves to be highly *inefficient* for your organization. It can also create deleterious consequences for the salespeople, themselves. In my work with wholesale distribution companies, internal surveys often reveal high levels of work stress among salespeople, who frequently feel that they "have too much to do in the time available." Given the wide range of tasks sales people are typically expected to complete, this should come as no surprise.

Increasing the division of labor and specialization around sales can reduce stress for your salespeople and increase your company's efficiency. This model, introduced by Justin Roff-Marsh (2015) in *The Machine,* has been embraced by innovative wholesale distributors. At its core, increasing sales specialization entails moving the responsibility for generating and qualifying leads to specialists who focus solely on doing so. These individuals, who are typically salaried, build and run systems that generate leads more efficiently than most salespeople can. Another specialist then sets appointments with qualified leads, on the salesperson's calendar. The efficiency gains come not only from this increased division of labor and specialization but also from the fact that the skilled lead specialists typically generate highly-targeted leads for salespeople.

This division of labor frees the salespeople to focus on sales presentations and to become exceptionally skilled at converting prospects through those presentations. Part and parcel of this process is moving salespeople away from *relationship selling* by providing them with *business reasons* for prospective customers to do business with you. As a young salesman, I spent much of my early career focused on the concept of *relationship selling*. At its core, relationship selling rests on a recognition that we don't really have anything from a business standpoint to offer the customer that differentiates ourselves. Instead, we have a sales model. In many companies, relationship selling just comes down to the customers' liking our salesperson better than the salesperson of our competitor—and we hope that will win the day. Clearly, that proposition proves risky, particularly because it means that, if the salesperson leaves, his or her customers may follow. That's not good for your company.

Let's consider this concept of relationship selling in the context of Max Weber's analysis of bureaucracy. Remember that Weber situated the rise of bureaucracy in the broader transformation of society from one dominated by *personal relationships* into one increasingly governed by *rational principles* and *economic transactions.* When we consider that Weber produced this analysis in the 19th century, we notice that **the sales role, as it currently exists in wholesale distribution, resembles an economic model of the 18th and 19th centuries.**

How can you move beyond that model to "rationalize" sales in your organization? By implementing Concierge Customer Service so that you can transform prospects to customers who will remain loyal, buy more from you, and make transaction decisions based not just upon personal feelings but also upon rational assessment. That's how you move sales in your organization from a 19th- to a 21st-century model.

But don't stop there. The **market penetration** function, which transforms money-*losing* accounts into money-*making* accounts, also represents a form of rationalization. The accounts that sit mired at the bottom of your profitability ranking report cost you money because their high volume comes with a correspondingly high cost to serve. That high cost to serve overwhelms the gross profit that the accounts produce. As we introduced earlier, "reforming" those accounts can be as simple as having your salespeople invite them to become platinum accounts by meeting platinum logistical requirements, so they receive the Concierge Customer Service that will make their lives easier and their businesses more profitable. Your salespeople, then, provide a rational basis for the behavior change. They might explain to less-profitable customers that, "The problem that we have right now is your account is out of balance because we're delivering things too frequently, in too-small quantities, and that's destroying your ability to be profitable and our ability to provide the service that we provide to other companies."

One of our clients identified a "mid-tier" of customers who were of sufficient size to generate much greater profit than they were currently generating. By articulating clearly both the requirements to qualify for Concierge Customer Service and the benefits for the customer of making these changes, they converted a number of accounts from money-losing to money-making status. And, because they then reported quarterly to these customers on the benefits the customers had received, in terms of problems solved and money saved by the Concierge Customer Service representatives, these customers continued to contribute to the company's bottom line.

Retaining Your Profitable Customers

As you change your orientation to customer service and put in place systems to monitor customer satisfaction and expectations across the board, you will increasingly garner the conversion, penetration, and retention gains. Now that you understand how you can fund your Concierge Customer Service system, let's delve into the 3 phases of implementing Concierge Customer Service.

"If you don't know where you're going, you'll end up someplace else." – Yogi Berra

CHAPTER 4: Phase I of Concierge Customer Service, The Customer and Team View

Now that you understand the advantages of Concierge Customer Service, how to finance it, and how to identify the right candidates, it's time to implement. The first thing to understand is the importance of customization. *You must tailor the system to your organization, your team, and your customers.* Although the core principles of Concierge Customer Service and customer-centric innovation do apply to all businesses, becoming customer-centric means, by definition, that you must adapt the Concierge Customer Service system to *your* customers. To do so, you must understand, from your customers' point of view, what kind of service they *want* and tailor your service to their preferences. In Phase I, you gather the requisite information, following the dictum that **you can't serve your customers well if you don't know them well**. Once you get this information, you must not only use it to tailor your Concierge Customer Service system to your customers' preferences but also communicate this valuable information to your employees. Do this consistently, to ensure that customer experience remains front of mind to everyone in your organization.

Giving Your Customers the Service They Want

As a young girl, I saw clearly that my father loved people and was masterful in understanding who they were and what "made them tick." In our small-town environment of the 1960s, talking to his customers proved sufficient to provide the business intelligence that fueled his success. But times change. To put Concierge Customer Service in place in today's world, you have to first answer 2 critically important questions:

1. What do your customers want?
2. How satisfied are they with the extent to which you're giving them what they want?

The answers can't be your gut reaction . . . they must be data-driven. And unlike my father, you can't answer these two questions just by talking to your customers. You also can't count on your salespeople to tell you accurately what your customers want and how satisfied they are.

Why are conversations with customers and reports from salespeople inadequate—and likely misleading? *Because people are much less likely to tell you things you might not want to hear when you talk with them face-to-face than when you give them a chance to respond confidentially in a survey.*[6] Sociologists have a fancy name for that, *social desirability response.* Research clearly documents just how pervasive and how deleterious the effects of social desirability response can be, not only in

---

[6] Notice that we describe surveys as "confidential" rather than "anonymous." Anonymity means that you have no way of identifying particular respondents. With online surveys, responses are almost never anonymous. Confidentiality, on the other hand, means that you know the identity of respondents but also protect that identity.

telephone or face-to-face conversations but also in interviews. ***This means that if you talk with your customers, you will be far less likely to hear any negative feedback that you need to hear than if you use a confidential survey.*** Getting accurate feedback—good *and* bad—is critical not only to building and maintaining your Concierge Customer Service system but also to ensuring continuous process improvement in your organization.

The process of garnering *accurate* customer data has proved to be a major stumbling block for far too many wholesale distributors because many of you are still gathering intelligence the way my father did. Here are the problems that typically hamstring companies like yours:

1. As we alluded to above, many of you rely on feedback you hear at customer events, information from your salespeople, and other kinds of ***anecdotal evidence***[7] to understand customer sentiment and this leaves you vulnerable—you may not even realize just *how* vulnerable. Serving your customers well requires *systematic* feedback from your customers, gathered through well-crafted surveys.[8]

2. Even distributors who use surveys to measure customer sentiment typically don't have the tools that provide the data you need to protect your

---

[7] Anecdotal evidence comes from personal observations or stories and provides limited utility. The limitations stem not only from the fact that these data are often collected casually but also from the fact that, even when they are collected more systematically, they represent too small a number of cases to provide generalizability.

[8] Systematic feedback comes from a structured, scientific process that governs not only the method by which the data are collected but also the number of cases and the method by which those cases are selected.

profitability. You often rely on overall indicators, such as Net Promoter Scores, that cannot provide sufficient information to orient your customer service, ensure continuous process improvement, and fuel your marketing. Achieving these outcomes requires both general and specific satisfaction data, as well as measures of customer loyalty.

3. In addition to asking the *wrong questions*, many distributors have trouble getting *answers* from customers because you don't have the *right tools to elicit responses*.

To serve your customers effectively, you must avoid those problems so you can answer those two critical questions of (1) what your customers want and (2) how well you're giving them what they want. That's the purpose of Phase I—to answer those questions, systematically, ensuring that you understand at a deep level "what keeps your customers awake at night" and how well you're satisfying them right now. Then you will use the information, in Phase II, to customize your Concierge Customer Service system.

The Opportunity Generator and the Feedback Generator allow you to answer those two fundamental questions. By using these tools to answer those two questions, you not only place your Concierge Customer Service system on a firm foundation but also gather information that most of your competitors *won't* have. Then, when you couple those data with systematic feedback from your employees, you're ready to launch your Concierge Customer Service system.

Figure 4.1

ANSWERING THE TWO CRITICAL QUESTIONS

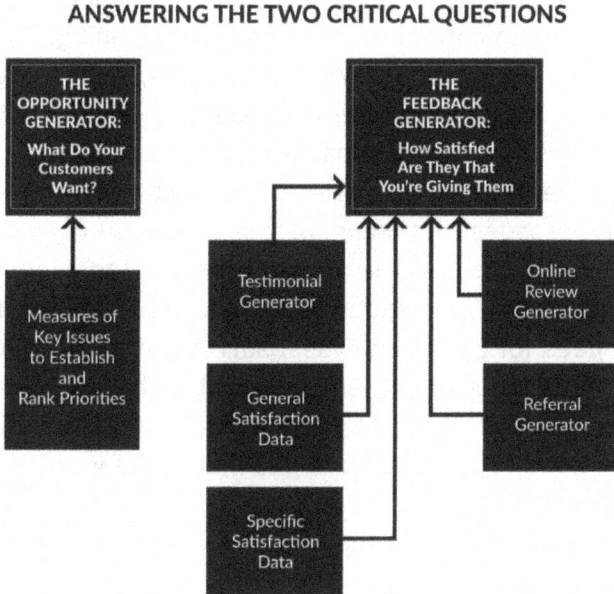

Using the Opportunity Generator to Know What Your Customers Want

One of the things we love most about working with wholesale distribution companies is your passion for serving your customers well. Despite that desire, many wholesale distributors struggle to understand, at a deep level, what the core concerns, challenges, and priorities of your customers really are. To make one thing abundantly clear, by "core concerns, challenges, and priorities," we aren't talking about their concerns vis-à-vis your business but instead about *their* concerns and challenges, writ large.

To clarify, let's think about what a consultant has to know about his or her prospective clients. Suppose this consultant specializes in identifying the issues that companies need to correct in their strategic planning. The tools she or he uses include SWOT (strengths, weaknesses, opportunities, and threats) analyses, surveys, and predictive analytics. If that consultant wants to attract and convert a larger number of qualified prospects, crafting marketing messages that focus on these tools is unlikely to work well. Why? Because the decision-makers the consultant wants to attract don't lie awake at night thinking about the need for SWOT analyses, surveys, or predictive analytics. What *does* keep them awake at night is

1. The desire to generate more leads who are qualified,
2. The need to convert more qualified leads into customers,
3. A focus on retaining their best (most profitable) customers,
4. The need to maintain overall profitability, and
5. The ongoing challenges of dealing with increasingly complex competition and technological change.

If I'm a smart consultant, I will orient my products and services, my content marketing, and my marketing messages around *those five issues*. Once I understand that these are the "hot-button issues" for my market, the rest becomes easy.

That's exactly what you need to do. Once you accomplish this, you can provide the customer service that your customers truly want and also gain the added bonus of knowing how to orient your products or services so they appeal to your customers, how to craft marketing messages that convert prospects to customers and customers to raving fans, and how to create content marketing that helps you not only retain your current customers but also attract more customers who are like them.

The Opportunity Generator opens a window to your customers' biggest concerns, priorities, or challenges and the problems they want to solve most urgently, giving you insight into what truly "keeps them awake at night." The direct benefit of this information for your Concierge Customer Service system clearly lies in your ability to ensure that you meet—and hopefully exceed—their customer service expectations. By doing so, you can increase both customer retention and customer spend by focusing squarely on issues that you know are most relevant. Take a look at Figure 4.2, on the next page, to see how simple and clean the data can be.

Figure 4.2

Sample Opportunity Generator Data					
Topics	Highest priority	High priority, but not highest	Somewhat of a priority	Not a priority at all	Highest priority + High priority
Ensuring the quality of your work	55%	40%	4%	1%	95%
Managing the workload in your business	60%	32%	5%	3%	92%
Decreasing your costs	59%	31%	6%	4%	90%
Ensuring consistency in timing of deliveries/ number of on-time deliveries	42%	44%	11%	3%	86%
Increasing your efficiency	40%	45%	10%	5%	85%
Marketing your business	30%	45%	20%	5%	75%
Being able to do all aspects of ordering from one online platform	26%	44%	23%	7%	70%
Improving training for your personnel	22%	44%	10%	24%	66%
Reducing back orders/delayed products	21%	44%	27%	8%	65%
Dealing with technological change	18%	34%	34%	14%	52%

Understanding the "hot button issues" in your market also becomes a key differentiator in your market. Most wholesale distributors fail to create content marketing because they simply don't know what to create, which opens an opportunity for you. Once your Opportunity Generator provides a list of the top 5 or 10 concerns of your customers, based upon the quantitative data, creating a content calendar becomes a simple matter of crafting messaging that address those issues and distributing the messages across the social media channels that your customers use most frequently. Doing so is integrally related to customer service because it provides another channel through which to enhance your bond with your customer, by providing the information he or she needs. The Opportunity Generator data can also open the door to beginning an email conversation with your customers—a conversation that most customers are eager to have but distributors are often reluctant to begin or maintain.

Of course, one of the key issues you should measure with the Opportunity Generator is the customer service touch points that prove most important to your customers. For example,

- How do they prefer to order? Ask them to choose the top 2 ways (response options may include on the phone, via fax, via text, through email, online, etc.).
- How do they prefer to communicate with you? Ask them to choose the top 2 ways (response options may include on the phone, via fax, via text, through email, online, etc.).
- How quickly do they expect quotes or answers to their questions? Response options might include within an hour, within 2-4 hours, within a business day, and within 2-3 business days.

When we've measured these kinds of customer preferences, the data have proved invaluable. One of the things to note with these data is the variation you will likely find in customer service and order preferences. For example, we find that Millennials increasingly want to text orders to distributors, whereas older cohorts often prefer to phone or email their orders. Once you have these data in hand, you can easily take them into your CRM to tag customer records, so you know exactly how to meet the specific preferences of specific customers. This type of segmentation can produce huge efficiency gains.

The Feedback Generator: How Well Are You Giving Your Customers What They Want?

Working in tandem with the Opportunity Generator, the Feedback Generator provides information on your customers' satisfaction and loyalty. These data prove critically important for two reasons. First, they illuminate areas in which you need to improve and in which customer service problems are likely to arise—if you can improve in those areas, you can reduce customer problems and complaints. Second, these data provide a baseline measure of satisfaction and loyalty against which to measure the results of your customer service and Concierge Customer Service efforts, in Phase III (where you turn your Opportunity Generator and Feedback Generator into an ongoing feedback system). Here, too, you gain added value because you can leverage this same information in your marketing, to **skyrocket conversions** externally; and to **ensure continuous process improvement** and **retention of your best customers,** internally.

Your ability to achieve these outcomes comes from the five core forms of data that your Feedback Generator provides:

1. Testimonials,
2. General satisfaction data,
3. Specific satisfaction data,
4. Referrals, and

5. Online reviews.

The first form of feedback you should gain from your Feedback Generator is **testimonials,** which provide you with anecdotal accounts of customer interactions that can also serve as the "stories that stick" with your customers and your prospective customers.[9] If you understand what your customers want and deliver it well, testimonials should flow easily but only *if* you also have a system to garner them effectively. In working with clients, I employ a proprietary Testimonial Generator that automatically invites a customer to leave a testimonial when he or she has provided positive feedback in one of the general satisfaction measures. I then ask for permission to use the testimonial, right inside the survey, so that the client can put that testimonial to work immediately on the company's website, in social media, and in marketing materials. You can gather literally hundreds of testimonials, with permission to use them, quickly and easily. This represents a key tool in building trust among customers (to bolster retention) and among prospective customers (to increase conversion).

If the satisfaction question reveals that the customer *isn't* happy, your system must forego the testimonial request and instead ask why the customer isn't satisfied— then **automatically send an email alert to your customer service team, so you can contact the customer quickly and correct the problem immediately.** Thus, you not only generate powerful testimonials that increase conversion but also increase

---

[9] These testimonials prove most powerful when they describe the problem or situation your customer had, before using your product or service; the experience of working with you; and the results they achieved.

retention by ensuring that you spot problems quickly and respond immediately. This is key to providing Concierge Customer Service.

But no matter how glowing your testimonials are, they can't give you a full picture of what your customers think. Moreover, customers and prospects alike may worry that the testimonials were hand-picked or don't represent typical results. The stark reality is that many of your competitors won't have the information to answer those questions or overcome those *objections*. **Statistical satisfaction data** provide the most powerful form of feedback to overcome that hurdle. And, when you combine the data with testimonials, you gain the ability to appeal to customers' and prospects' logic and to their emotions.

General satisfaction data come from measures in the Customer Feedback Generator that tap the global, or overall satisfaction with your product, service, or business. These measures typically provide useful information for your marketing because they're easily interpreted and offer a summary indicator. For example, they can tell you the percentage of customers who would recommend you or indicate the percentage of customers who are very satisfied, somewhat satisfied, somewhat dissatisfied, and very dissatisfied with your business. The former measure, the percentage who would recommend you to a competitor, taps not only satisfaction but also loyalty. You must measure both loyalty and satisfaction because satisfaction is a necessary but not sufficient condition for customer loyalty: Satisfied customers can, and do, walk.

These data can prove immensely powerful for your business. Suppose you find that 96% of your customers are satisfied but 25% of them are only "somewhat satisfied." Those data reveal two important things. First, they provide a wonderful statistic that you can use in your marketing, because 96% satisfaction is certainly something that will impress prospective customers. **But you've also identified a potential threat: The fact that fully 1 in 4 of your customers prove to be only "somewhat satisfied" indicates that you're falling short in some way**. The question you must answer—quickly and accurately—is *where* you're falling short.

Figure 4.3

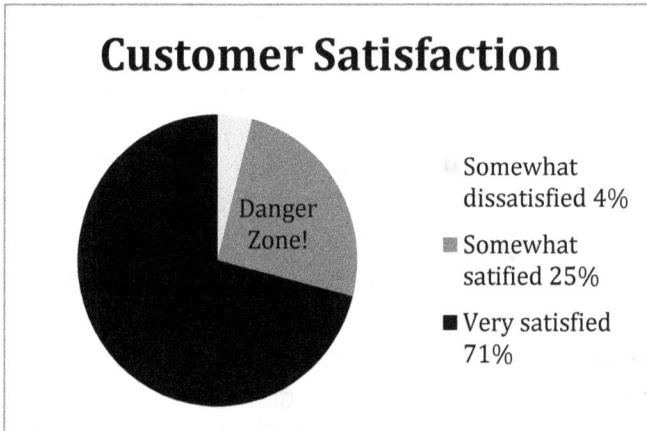

Customer Satisfaction

Danger Zone!

Somewhat dissatisfied 4%

Somewhat satified 25%

Very satisfied 71%

Answering that question requires that you supplement the general satisfaction data with **specific satisfaction data. Specific satisfaction data** augment the general or overall data in 2 ways. First, if overall satisfaction proves to be high, the specific measures illuminate areas that can still be enhanced—and those data can help you understand how to move more customers from "somewhat satisfied" to "very satisfied." We often deliver to our clients data that show extremely high levels of overall satisfaction, yet the specific measures still illuminate opportunities for improvement. For example, one of our clients was delighted to discover that more than 95% of their customers were satisfied, but we were also able to show them that their customers wanted better ecommerce and online ordering capabilities. ***This represented a huge opportunity for the company, because it provided a way in which they could reduce costs for the customers who did not qualify for Concierge Customer Service.*** In other cases, we find that salespeople are not suggesting additional products or services that might be useful for a given customer. Uncovering that pattern reveals another pathway to greater profit.

The second way in which specific satisfaction data prove invaluable is when overall satisfaction proves to be *low*. In that case, the specific satisfaction measures provide vital information to identify critical areas of improvement—including customer service—on which you can take action to increase overall satisfaction *before* it affects your bottom line. Imagine, for example, if you discovered that only 80% of your customers were satisfied and 20%—fully 1 in 5—were dissatisfied.

Figure 4.4

Customer Satisfaction

Danger Zone!

Satisfied 80%
Dissatisfied 20%

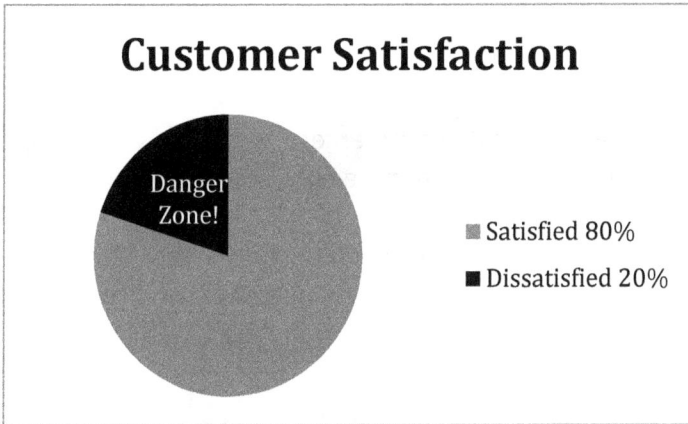

Or suppose you relied solely on a Net Promoter score to measure satisfaction and you discovered that 30% of your customers fell into the "detractor" category. Without specific satisfaction data, you would have no way of knowing where to focus, to improve overall satisfaction. Specific measures solve that problem for you by revealing the areas on which your customers feel you are falling short. Obviously, it's critically important to use these measures to tap:

- The level of satisfaction with customer service,
- Customers' perceptions of the degree to which customer service representatives advocate for the customers,
- The extent to which customers perceive customer service representatives to be (a) friendly and (b) professional, and
- The customers' perceived ability to get to the right person immediately when a problem arises.

Other key areas to tap with specific satisfaction measures can include:

- Measures of satisfaction with delivery accuracy and timing;
- Your website and ecommerce;
- Their ability to find items easily;
- Product availability;
- How knowledgeable the sales team is about your products and the customer's business, respectively; and
- Pricing.

> *Here's the bottom line: What determines whether you can retain a customer is what THEY believe happened in their interactions with you.* One of the most important observations in social science was made by W.I Thomas, who stressed that "if men perceive situations as real, they are real in their consequences" (Merton, 1995). So regardless of whether *you* believe you serve your customers well, you have to understand what *they* believe. That is why it is so important to consistently measure customer satisfaction with both types of measures.

These general and specific satisfaction measures also fuel your marketing by providing even more ammunition to increase conversions, sales, and revenue. To make them even more powerful, make sure you include specific satisfaction questions that cover areas in which customers' objections typically arise, to gain a powerful weapon for overcoming those objections.

Another opportunity that your Feedback Generator can provide, one most distributors miss, is using it to generate **referrals** inside your surveys. Referrals come most easily when you **invite** satisfied customers to refer their connections to you. Remember the homophily principle that we discussed earlier: Because your customers' connections are highly likely to be similar to your current customers—your ideal target market—and because your customers' connections are much more likely to trust you if they receive a referral directly from someone they know and trust, conversions on referrals are extraordinarily high. **The Referral Generator is the tool that lets you glean easily the referrals that Concierge Customer Service creates and provides an indicator of how well your Concierge Customer Service system is making you referable.**

The fourth benefit your Feedback Generator must provide is **online reviews.** Although online reviews often lie "off the radar" for wholesale distributors, these reviews have become a key driver in consumer decision-making: Remember the study by Deloitte, which reveals that 1 in 4 (25%) of all Americans do "comparison shopping" on the web and fully 75%—3 in 4—of surveyed respondents indicated that the information presented on online rating sites is "generally fair (Keckley and Coughlin, 2012)." **This means that the decision-makers in the companies you serve will increasingly turn to these reviews.** In fact, we've found online reviews that some wholesale distributors' customers have placed online—and the distributors didn't even know they were there. Because so many distributors underestimate the importance of these reviews, those who do implement a system—like the Online Review Generator—to ethically encourage positive reviews can quickly move ahead of competitors who don't take action. We use a system that can automatically invite a customer who says they would recommend your business to leave a comment on your Facebook or LinkedIn page and open a window to that page. If you're providing Concierge Customer Service to your customers, satisfied customers can automatically be invited to leave online reviews with an Online Review Generator.

Other Areas to Measure

You should also tap into key preferences and expectations that will inform the design of your Concierge Customer Service system. These should include the customers' top choices for contacting a CSR or CCSR, how quickly they expect a response and/or quote from a CSR or CCSR, and what kinds of functions they would like to conduct online (e.g., checking invoices, paying bills, tracking deliveries, etc.).

Getting Response

As we mentioned above, most wholesale distributors encounter difficulty getting customers to respond to their surveys. Response proves critical to ensuring that you represent accurately your customers' opinions: The greater the proportion of customers who respond, the more representative your results become. Here are steps to improving response:

1. **ALWAYS provide an incentive**. You might, for example, invite your customers with a promise that everyone who completes the questions will earn a chance to win one of ten $100 Amazon gift cards. The investment you make will prove well worth it when you put your data to work—and you will build good will with your customers by showing them that you value their time and input.

2. **Use multiple invitations**. If you choose to conduct your survey online (which is what we recommend, because of practicality and cost), it is imperative to send multiple email invitations, not only because it increases response but also because you tend to draw different portions of the population across the three invitations.[10]

3. **Craft a good survey**. Unfortunately, many—perhaps most—surveys that companies send out fail because they (a) include poorly-constructed questions and (b) imply that the whole purpose of the survey is to serve the interests of the *business*, not the interests of the *customer*. If your *business* is customer-centric, then your survey certainly must be. Make it feel as if it's about the *customer*, not about you or your company. Do that by offering an incentive, by keeping it short, by focusing it squarely on the customer, and by promising the customer, in

---

[10] The first invitation typically draws the most enthusiastic customers, either because they prove to be highly positive or because they are strongly negative. The second and third invitations tend to bring in respondents who lie more in the center of the distribution.

the introduction, that you will use the information to serve him or her more effectively.

Spreading the Word

Once you have these data in hand, you not only need to put them to work internally and use them in your marketing but also communicate them clearly to your employees. As we outline in Chapter 5, you should communicate the results of your Phase I customer survey—both the items you can celebrate and the opportunities for improvement—with your employees. One of the best ways to do that is via a webinar or some other type of presentation that you can record. This way, employees who cannot access the presentation live can still view the material and they can also return to the material later, as needed.

And don't miss the opportunity to communicate your Phase I results to your customers. To do so, create a one-page report that reports on 3-5 key findings in the data. Here's how we suggest you structure the report:

1. Thank them for providing their feedback and making the project a HUGE success.
2. Note that you awarded the survey incentives (for example, 10 gift cards) to happy winners.
3. Note that you listened to and learned from what they told you by not only performing a careful analysis of the data but also by reading every single comment that they shared with you, so you can act on it appropriately.
4. Summarize 3-5 key data findings:

a. Begin with areas in which you excelled. For most of our clients, the overall satisfaction measures ("How satisfied are you with XXX, overall" and "How likely would you be to recommend XXX to another company who was not a direct competitor of yours?") provide high marks.

b. Thank them for the praise; then promise them that you will work to live up to their confidence in you.

c. Next, turn to your opportunities for improvement. For example, if they told you that they're far less satisfied with your ecommerce, website, and email communication than they are with your customer service and delivery, report that to them and tell them how you'll take action to capitalize upon the opportunities for improvement that they illuminated for you.

By doing this, you've shown your customers that you *listen* to what they tell you and *take action on their input.* Doing so will differentiate your company in the marketplace because very, very few companies report back to their customers in this way after the company conducts a survey. This helps to strengthen the all-important bond with your customers, which lies at the foundation not only of customer service but also of your very business. It also helps to "train" your customers to respond to your surveys by showing them that you will, indeed, act on their input.

Here are some other important ways to use these Phase I data:

1. Feed your survey data regularly into a dashboard, to allow you to disseminate visuals that can compare satisfaction across customer segments (for example, between those who do and do not receive Concierge Customer Service), identify trends in satisfaction levels, trigger "hot button" issues with your customer service, and the like.

2. Generate reports that highlight both good and bad results in your customer surveys. Make sure to congratulate your employees on their accomplishments and identify clear action items/plans where satisfaction falls below threshold levels.

3. Invite your employees to comment and share insights on the survey results, particularly where you may have unanticipated findings.

The "Other Side" of Phase I Feedback: Eliciting Input from Your Team

As we established in Chapter 2, ensuring customer satisfaction depends upon ensuring employee satisfaction. That is why Phase I of your Concierge Customer Service journey should also include a survey of your employees. Remember, one of the key reasons for conducting an online survey, rather than speaking directly to someone, is to avoid "social desirability response,"[11] to increase the accuracy of the feedback.

Here are some of the key items to include in your internal survey:

1. **Employees' perception of customers' overall satisfaction and satisfaction with customer service**: We often find a gap between employees' perceptions of customers' satisfaction and the actual satisfaction. In some cases, they overestimate customer satisfaction and in others, they estimate it to be too low. If they overestimate customer satisfaction, it becomes extremely important to show employees both the opportunity for improvement and the need for the employees to review quantitative measures of satisfaction routinely (this is one reason that data dashboards can prove extremely useful). If they underestimate customer satisfaction, this provides a golden opportunity in which to bolster morale by demonstrating the team is creating even greater customer satisfaction than they realized.

2. **Valued job characteristics:** Remember that the best way to measure employee satisfaction is by tapping the extent to which employees perceive that the job characteristics they value are present in their jobs. So tap the extent to which they desire pay, growth opportunities, coworker relationships, work resources, and the like.

---

[11] As we described above, social desirability response occurs when individuals alter their survey responses when in the presence of an interviewer.

3. **Satisfaction with valued characteristics:** Using the same set of attributes, measure the how satisfied employees are with the extent to which those characteristics are present in their jobs.

4. **Overall job satisfaction:** In addition to measuring the extent to which valued job characteristics are present, we also suggest that you include an overall job satisfaction measure. Rather than asking how satisfied employees are with their jobs, overall, we recommend that you ask how likely they would be to recommend a job at your company to a friend or relative.

5. **Work stress:** Understanding the degree to which employees perceive stress in their work, and how that perception varies across individuals and departments, provides important information. One of the best single indicators of work stress is, "How much of the time do you feel you have too much to do in the time available?" Notably, we often find high levels of work stress among salespeople, likely because of the diverse scope of their roles and tasks.

6. **Perception of website, ecommerce, and related areas:** Even among distributors with exceptionally high levels of satisfaction, we often find lower levels of satisfaction with the website, ecommerce, and related areas. For that reason, we suggest that you ask specifically about employees' perceptions of these tools.

Knowing Them Well

In Phase I of Concierge Customer Service, then, you gather baseline data from both your customers and your employees. If you execute these simple steps well and continually, you'll have the foundation you need to ensure that you always know your customers (and your employees) well. In the next chapter, we show you how to use that information to ensure you serve them well.

"Merely satisfying customers will not be enough to earn their loyalty. Instead, they must experience exceptional service worthy of their repeat business and referral. Understand the factors that drive this customer revolution." – Rick Tate

CHAPTER 5: Phase II, Putting Your CCS System in Place

By now, you understand the core premise: With Concierge Customer Service, you can give your best customers the edge they're looking for and improve *your* profits in the process. **Concierge Customer Service (CCS)** achieves that goal by giving your most profitable customers a level of service that not only makes their lives and jobs easier but also improves their efficiency. That's why CCS proves to be such a win-win for your company: Because the CCS system provides your top customers with such profit-generating perks as

- fast and efficient problem resolution,
- priority call on inventory, and
- preferred pricing,

the benefits of the system flow to your customers' bottom lines **and** to yours. Your company can differentiate itself in the marketplace by making a new, compelling **business case** for working with you. You will create a marketplace bias toward your company, one that is rooted in rationality and reason rather than personality and emotion. Now that we understand the concept, we get down to the "nuts and bolts" of implementation.

Step 1 to Customer-Centric Innovation

The first step in implementing Concierge Customer Service is to get everyone on your team involved with and committed to the program. This begins with communicating to your employees the results of both the customer (external) and employee (internal) surveys from Phase I and also the overall nature of the program. You frame the introduction of the program with your customers' and employees' feedback. We recommend that you communicate the information via webinar: The advantage of that format is that you can record the presentation, making it easy for employees who cannot view the presentation live to access it later on. It also permits those who need to see it a second (or third) time to do so on demand.

We generally break the material into 3 separate webinars:

- **Webinar 1**: Review with your employees your Phase I customer survey results. Highlight in the review
    - o The items to celebrate—be sure to congratulate employees on these achievements and consider providing some sort of reward for them.
    - o The opportunities for improvement. Here, we suggest that you include action items and solicit input and insights from your employees on how to capitalize upon your improvement opportunities.
- **Webinar 2:** Review with your employees the internal survey results.

- o   Here, too, you should highlight both the positive findings and the opportunities for improvement.
- o   Employee insights can prove particularly valuable in providing context and detail that will help you not only understand the findings better but also devise action plans. For example, if you find that employee engagement isn't as high as you would like or that employees do not perceive that they are given sufficient resources to do their jobs, employee insights can prove very valuable in understanding and responding to these findings.
- **Webinar 3:** Introduce your Concierge Customer Service program to your employees. Begin by outlining the intent and goals of the program (you can use material from chapters 1 and 2 of this book to help frame this discussion). Then, provide particulars on how and by whom the program will be implemented (use material from this chapter to frame that discussion).
  - o   Once you have run the webinars, make the recordings available.

Step 2: The CCSR Job Description

Your next step will be to craft your Concierge Customer Service Representative (CCSR) job description. Here are some of the core elements that you *may* include, depending on how you structure sales and customer service responsibilities:

1. The CCSR serves as the first point of contact for all levels of customers who receive Concierge Customer Service.
2. The CCSR will provide information about the company's products and services, handle customer relations, respond to quote requests, deal with customers' issues and/or technical problems, deal with delivery problems, and process orders.[12]
3. The CCSR will build personal relationships with customers and provide superior service at all times.
4. The CCSR will not just respond to customer complaints but work actively to build, maintain, and deepen customer relationships. *The CCSR should strive to make each Concierge Customer Service customer feel as if he or she is the only customer in the world.*

A CCSR should bring a minimum of 2 years of customer service and/or sales experience, preferably in the wholesale distribution industry. The ideal educational background lies in business, communications, psychology, or sociology.[13] Because the CCSRs work with your largest, most valuable customers, business-to-business experience is highly desirable.

Because the CCSR will be the first line of contact between the customers and your company, the most

---

[12] In most cases, it's advisable to shift order taking to sales, whenever possible (see chapter 3 regarding reorganization of sales and customer service).

[13] Other undergraduate degrees, including humanities, can also be appropriate if the individual also brings business experience and/or additional business training.

important qualification of the CCSR will be his or her communication and, in particular, listening skills. The CCSR must be able to adapt quickly and easily to changing situations and be a quick learner; he or she must have a growth, as opposed to a fixed mindset. He or she must be able to make informed decisions quickly and feel empowered to serve the customer better. She or he should also possess good organizational skills. Other qualifications to look for are computer literacy, a friendly personality, and attention to detail.

Step 3: Recruiting

Filling CCSR position(s) by promoting from within can be a strategy that reduces training time and also boosts employee morale: Employees will recognize potential for growth in your company, which leads to increased commitment and motivation toward their jobs. If you plan to recruit a CCSR internally, begin by identifying high-potential employees. Place your "superstars" immediately at the top of the candidate list. Performance evaluations, customer feedback, measures of achieved sales,[14] ranking systems (such as 9-box) or 360 evaluations can all help you identify exceptional internal candidates. Tools like these can streamline the screening process, expediting the development of a candidate pool.

If recruiting externally, ensure that you have a hiring system in place. Launching the Concierge Customer Service

---

[14] If you move salespeople into this position, the best strategy generally lies in assigning individuals who work well with customers and understand them horoughly, but do not excel in actual selling.

program offers a great opportunity to review your hiring process to ensure that it works well. Know which sites create applicant flow and have a trained person who screens resumes. Once you identify a resume as being viable, conduct a brief phone screening of the applicant, to ensure that the applicant brings the requisite experience and that the salary range is acceptable to him or her. This helps to avoid wasting time on over- or under-qualified candidates. Applicants who move successfully through that screening should go through a behavioral-based interview with the hiring manager, using open-ended questions (for example, "Tell me about a time when you..."). This will allow the hiring manager to not only to hear how the applicant has acted in the past (because past behavior strongly predicts future behavior) but also to see how well the candidate can sell him- or herself. The CCSR should be provided with a copy of your company's employee handbook and any other relevant materials, so she or he can become familiar with these documents. Because the CCSR will serve as a spokesperson for the company, she or he should be able to reference these materials. The advantage of bringing in a CCSR candidate from outside lies primarily in the opportunity to garner new ideas and/or perspectives.

Although personality testing and profiling are not requisite, we strongly suggest that you use these resources to help you identify the candidate(s) who fit the CCSR position well. One key personality characteristic that proves essential in a customer service role is social sensitivity—the ability to read and react to people's emotions appropriately. When selecting candidates, bear in mind that you can teach technical skills but you cannot teach personality.

Such personality tests as Kolbe-A,™ Myers-Briggs, or the DiSC® assessment provide affordable assessment options to measure personality traits and orientations. Where possible, hiring a profiler who can not only administer a battery of assessments but also provide detailed interpretation of them can prove to be a worthwhile investment, particularly if that profiler works personally with your team (rather than simply delivering results). As with all employees, the CCSR should receive an appropriate onboarding experience. This should include the basic orientation process (such as new hire paperwork, review of company policies, safety training, etc). In addition to the standard orientation, the CCSR's introduction should include personal interaction with all relevant stakeholders. As mentioned before, the CCSR will need to know all aspects of the business to serve the customers efficiently and will also need to maintain good working relationships with individuals in other departments. It becomes critical, then, for him or her to develop inter-departmental relationships early.[15]

Step 4: Identifying Candidates for Concierge Customer Service

Once you create the job description and structure for your human resources system, the next step is to develop the criteria that will qualify customers for this level of service. As we outlined in Chapter 3, if you use WayPoint profit analytics, the candidates for Concierge Customer

---

[15] If your internal survey in Phase I identified issues or problems regarding how internal employees cooperate (in other words, if information and/or cooperation are not as strong across the departments as they should be), we advise strongly that you address these issues before instituting Concierge Customer Service.

Service should come from the High Leverage and High Efficiency accounts. We do not recommend inviting all of these accounts to your Concierge Customer Service program in the beginning of your program. As you implement the program, the best way to introduce the process in a way that minimizes "hiccups" is to begin with 25-30 of your best customers. Introduce the program to them in the ways that we outline below and elicit feedback about the program within 3 months. From that feedback, you identify any gaps or deficiencies in the program and also elicit testimonials and statistical data that document the program's benefits: These testimonials can prove particularly beneficial for your salespeople, as they recruit competitors of your top customers by highlighting the benefits of Concierge Customer Service. This is the way in which you can "clone" your best customers and provide a business case to your salespeople for doing so. Then, you are free to expand the program to more of your High Leverage and High Efficiency accounts.

Step 5: Codifying the Structure of Your Concierge Customer Service System

In most cases, we suggest dedicating at least 2 representatives to your Concierge Customer Service customers. Where resources don't permit that structure, you can install a single CCSR who will be "backed up" by at least one Customer Service Representative (who has been trained thoroughly in the Concierge Customer Service system). The reason for this structure is to ensure that, when a CCS customer calls in, he or she will be reach a representative quickly. In no case should a CCS customer be routed to an automated menu. We recommend that you establish a dedicated Concierge Customer Service phone number that you provide to all CCS customers; one wonderful way to do that is to give CCS customers a gift— such as an iPad case, phone holder, or similar item—that bears your logo and the dedicated CCS phone number.

Although this is the preferred structure, the principle is not inviolable. We have worked with companies who discovered that their top customers preferred to remain with the customer service representative with whom they were currently working, rather than shifting to a dedicated CCSR. In that case, the company generally trains all of their CSRs as CCSRs, establishing a system in which the company ensures that Concierge Customer Service customers have priority in reaching representatives. *Remember: The goal is to give customers an exceptional level of service but to do so in a way that corresponds to the customers' preferences.*

As they work with and solve problems for customers, CCSRs should record their interactions with customers, documenting clearly

- what problems the customer presented,
- who presented the problem (company, position, and name/contact information),
- the actions taken, and
- the outcome.

We recommend that you report to CCS customers monthly, or at least quarterly, on the actions taken; where possible, identify in these reports savings of time or money created for the customer. Doing so ensures that your customers recognize and remain aware of the benefits that they receive from your company.

Recording the nature of customer problems or complaints also serves another function: It provides quantitative data that show you exactly when and where problems arise—and many distributors lack these data. Once you begin collecting these data, you can identify key opportunities for improvement; taking action in these areas allows you to reduce customer complaints, improve customer satisfaction, and decrease costs. Ideally, you should have a dashboard that not only displays customer feedback data but also provides a mechanism for CSRs and CCSRs to code customer complaints/problems. This allows CCSRs to keep their pulse on both customer sentiment and customer issues.

CCSRs should also monitor customer accounts and relationships closely so that they can act to mitigate problems *before* they arise. If, for example, a CCSR recognizes that a recently-ordered product is backordered, he or she should act to minimize negative effects of the situation (by, perhaps, sending a substitute product at no cost to the customer). Because of the importance of this and other functions, CCSRs should have access to your CRM and understand clearly how to use it to perform their roles.

Step 6: Identifying Concierge Customer Service Benefits

Your next step should be to identify the benefits of Concierge Customer Service, clearly and specifically. We've already identified some of the key benefits, which include a special phone number that connects the CCS customer directly with his or her CCSR. Here are some of the other things you might consider offering to Concierge Customer Service customers:

1. Priority call on inventory;
2. Expedited shipping when necessary;
3. Reporting on order status;
4. Expedited quotes;
5. Entertainment opportunities (such as tickets to sporting or cultural events), where allowed;
6. Greeting cards for birthdays and other occasions (CCSRs may need access to your CRM for this function);
7. Offering customers continuous improvement opportunities.

After you codify the benefits and the exact nature of your system, you should create a matrix that lists (a) each benefit that CCS customers receive, (b) who in your organization "owns" responsibility for ensuring that this benefit is delivered,[16] and (c) each department/individual who is involved in delivery of that benefit. Where possible, build in redundancy to the system so that if a given individual can't provide the benefit, someone else will.

---

[16] In the majority of cases, the CCSR will bear responsibility for ensuring that each customer receives each benefit. However, in some cases, the organizations with whom we work task members of the executive team/C-suite with delivering certain benefits.

Step 7: Introducing Your Concierge Customer Service Program

Once you identify your top-priority accounts, hire personnel, and articulate the benefits of your system clearly, you should introduce your Concierge Customer Service program to eligible customers. First, create a brochure that outlines the benefits of the system and congratulates them on their acceptance to the program. This brochure should go ONLY to eligible customers. Next, we suggest that you create a video in which you introduce the CCSRs to CCS customers. Then, CCSRs should meet personally with each and every CCS customer, ensuring that the customers understand the benefits of the system and answering any questions that they may have.

Because Concierge Customer Service should serve as a tool through which your salespeople can recruit accounts that are similar to your current CCS customers, it becomes critically important to train your salespeople on the benefits of the program. We suggest that you create an internal brochure, similar to the one that you create for eligible customers, outlining program benefits. Then, create for your salespeople a list of target accounts—companies that resemble closely your CCS customers—and coach your salespeople on how to recruit these customers. As you do so, it's imperative to ensure that your salespeople understand that only some customers qualify for Concierge Customer Service and that they also understand clearly who qualifies and why.

Undoubtedly, customers who don't qualify for Concierge Customer Service will hear of the program and question why they are not receiving its benefits. That's your opportunity to "reform" customers who are currently not highly profitable: Making clear to them the activities that can make them eligible for CCS (for example, combining orders so that the cost to serve those customers declines) can provide a lever to turn an unprofitable customer into one that generates profit. Of course, not all customers have that potential, but some will. This is why it becomes so imperative that salespeople are crystal clear on the requirements for CCS eligibility.

Step 8: The CCSR Process

When a customer calls a CCSR with a problem or issue, the CCSRs should always use these steps in problem resolution:

1. Identify the problem;
2. Ask questions, to gather more information. For example, if the wrong product was delivered or a delivery was late, go through the sequence of events to ensure you know where the problem arose and how quickly it needs to be rectified;
3. Clearly document the conversation;
4. Summarize the problem to the customer, based upon what the CCSR has gleaned from the customer, to ensure the CCSR understands the customer's concerns;
5. Outline to the customer the steps that the CCSR will take to resolve the problem;
6. Give the customer a timeframe, and
7. Assure the customer that the agent will personally solve the problem—and then do so, apprising the customer of steps along the way.

Concierge Customer Service representatives must be trained thoroughly in these steps; before they assume the role, they must have demonstrated mastery of this process. Ensure that these steps are ensconced not only in your training but also in your Concierge Customer Service Representative manual. Management should monitor the data on problem resolution and customer feedback, to ensure the quality of the solution process.

Step 9: Goal Setting

CCSRs must continually learn and grow, and thus should work with their managers to set and achieve new goals. Ideally, the CCSR and his or her manager should revisit and revise goals at least quarterly. These goals should be SMART goals, where SMART stands for:

- **Specific** – Goals must be defined clearly, so that anyone who has a basic knowledge of the project can understand them.
- **Measurable** – Know if the goal is obtainable and how far away completion is; measure and document achievement of your goal.
- **Achievable** – Ensure that you provide the CCSR sufficient resources to achieve the goal.
- **Results-Oriented** – Have a clearly-identified outcome for your goal.
- **Time-Based** – Ensure that you have enough time to achieve the goal, but do not allow the period to stretch too far.

Step 10: Performance Evaluations, Turnover, and Retention

Performance evaluations benefit both employee and employer by providing an opportunity for meaningful conversation and constructive feedback. Both parties can set goals and expectations to improve future performance. Ongoing performance evaluations are necessary because they help to avoid serious problems or sub-optimal skill development. Review customer feedback data to understand customers' perceptions of CCSR performance.

Turnover can be costly for any position, but it can be particularly problematic (and costly to your organization) for the Concierge Customer Service representative. Because customers do not want a constant "changing of the guard" of CCSRs, it is important to ensure that your CCSR succeeds in his or her job and ensure that she or he prospers in a healthy workplace. Being aware of your employees and looking for cues that something could go wrong can help you fix a problem before it escalates. Treat the CCSR as an investment and valuable asset to the company—because losing these people will impact both the company and your customers.

Succession planning for CCSR positions should be ongoing. Planning in advance who is able to perform the CCSR duties will help minimize any interruptions in service, should a CCSR leave. Remember: Because these individuals work with your most profitable accounts, you must ensure that no interruption of Concierge Customer Service occurs. Potential employees should be identified and mentored so that they could step in at any time; they should be trained in the system and, if a CCSR does leave, the new representative should be introduced to the customer by the current CCSR.

Step 11: Feedback

Continuous improvement must be a hallmark of your company's culture. The data that you collected in Phase I help you to ensure continuous process improvement by showing you where opportunities for improvement lie. As you continue to collect those data, in Phase III, you must constantly monitor the data and glean the action items that will ensure continuous improvement. Equally important to continuous improvement is providing both negative and positive feedback to your team. An employee may not know he or she is doing something wrong and can learn and grow only through feedback. Conversely, a job well done should always be immediately recognized. Follow Southwest Airline's model (see Chapter 2) of looking for opportunities to reward employees for jobs done well.

Step 12: Internal Customer Service

As established in Chapter 2, employee satisfaction and engagement affect customer satisfaction, engagement, and loyalty. Therefore, we recommend that you designate an individual or a small team of employees as an internal customer service team. This team would work together to strengthen employee engagement and increase employee morale. Below is a list of actions this team may perform:

- Send out cards for special occasions, such as birthdays and work anniversaries.
- Plan lunches, social hours, or gatherings.
- Recognize employees and their accomplishments.

- Create an employee newsletter.
- Create employee assistance programs.

We also recommend that you remain attentive to the engagement and satisfaction of your employees, through ongoing measurement. Remember the material we introduced in Chapter 2. Harvard Business Review reports, "companies with highly engaged people outperform firms with the most disengaged folks—by 54% in employee retention, by 89% in customer satisfaction, and by fourfold in revenue growth" (Goffee and Jones, 2013).

Making Your System Work

You can see the steps to implementing Concierge Customer Service. The key to success lies in completing each of these steps so that you define the CCSR role clearly; identifying, hiring, and training the right CCSRs; outlining clearly both the qualifications and the benefits of the system, ensuring that you also identify everyone involved in delivering benefits; and constantly improving the system. In the next chapter, we show you how to gather and use data effectively, in Phase III.

"Earl's Dead—Cadillac for sale; Eldorado sits out on the Tamiami Trail. Sign on the windshield tells the whole tale, Earl's Dead—Cadillac for Sale." – Jimmy Buffett

CHAPTER 6: Keeping the Feedback Coming in Phase III and Mining Your Gold

The quote above comes from a talented storyteller. Although the line says that the "sign on the windshield tells the whole tale," it was Jimmy Buffett who took that single data point—a sign on a car that read, "Earl's Dead, Cadillac for Sale" —and used it to weave a fantastic tale of how Earl, the human cannonball, and his wife, Moonvine, towed Earl's cannon behind a Cadillac Eldorado, "down to Panama and back up to Maine" having so much fun that they "did it all again." Whether the single data point that grounded the story existed in fact or only in Jimmy Buffett's imagination, Buffett's talent lay in his ability to weave the story around the data.

And that's exactly where *your* untapped power lies, in being able to find and tell the story hiding in your data and using that story effectively. Finding and articulating that story proves to be part art and part science. The science lies in interpreting data accurately, ensuring that you find the story but never reach or even approach conclusions that exceed the limitations of the data. But there is an art to finding the story that lies within the numbers, skill that comes from both expertise and experience. The art lies in taking what the data *say*—with complete accuracy—and using that to articulate what they *mean*, separating the "forest from the trees" to tell a *compelling story.*

Caution! Doing that is not easy. Being able to really dig into data and understand what they mean, without overstating or understating the implications, takes science. But to really use data effectively—internally, to orient your customer service and ensure continuous process improvement, and externally in your marketing—you must tell the story that will move beyond the numbers to impel people to action.

How do you find and tell the story in your data? The first step is to understand that numbers, in and of themselves, can't tell the story for you. Here's an example. After Hurricane Katrina hit south Louisiana, I served on the Inter-Agency Performance Evaluation Task Force (IPET) for the US Army Corps of Engineers, on one of ten discipline-specific teams tasked with telling the story of the social consequences of the disaster. As a result of the work we did, I spent countless hours on the phone with reporters from inside and outside the US, who wanted to understand better what happened.

One question popped up repeatedly: Why didn't more people leave??

The answer to that question was actually pretty simple. It lay primarily in two statistics: The number of New Orleanians who lacked cars and the number who were caring for the aged and the infirm. Those numbers were large and I cited them repeatedly.

But to make people *care* about what happened, to make them *understand why people became trapped,* I had to do much more than just cite cold statistics. I had to use the numbers to tell a story—an accurate story, a true story that doesn't overreach the data, the story of what happened to those people who were left in New Orleans to suffer. So I began to unpack the numbers by explaining that thousands of people—many of whom were poor—had no cars. Thousands of others were caring for the ill or elderly and for them, transporting the people in their care proved difficult, if not impossible.

Add to those facts the reality that the "run-up" to Katrina was fast, making the time for preparation and evacuation was unusually short, and the situation becomes still more complex. Securing shelter and navigating out of the city often proved challenging, even for people with resources. Here's my story to illustrate. I walked into our house in Baton Rouge on the Friday afternoon before Katrina, found my husband sitting at the computer, and asked what he was doing. He said, "making reservations." "For what?" "For Katrina. It's headed this way." We *studied* the effects of hurricanes, we were *part* of the LSU Hurricane Center, yet up until that moment, I was completely unaware that this Category 5 storm[17] now held New Orleans in its sights. My husband fortunately secured 3 different hotel reservations in 3 different cities; by the next morning, there were no hotel reservations available between New Orleans and Memphis. In the end, we didn't evacuate but we gave our reservations to friends who had not been able to make reservations in time.

For those who didn't have the options and resources we had, the situation became very bleak, very quickly. The

---

[17] Katrina weakened to a Category 3 by its Gulf Coast landfall.

fact that people became trapped, either because they lacked transportation and had no way out or because they wouldn't leave behind those for whom they were caring, provides the core of the story behind the people evacuated to Houston and Idaho and other corners of the country, the story behind the horror in the Superdome and the Convention Center, the story behind the communities destroyed and the hundreds of lives lost in the storm. In these paragraphs, I gave you the data—but I wove them into a *story* about what happened.

Every business has a story. Your opportunity lies in being able to gather and understand data well, then use those data to tell your story effectively.

You must tell your story internally, to your team, ensuring that they know your customers so well that they understand exactly how to serve your customers well. That's how you motivate them to make your Concierge Customer Service system a success.

You must share your story with your customers, so they understand how well you're serving them and what benefits you provide to them. That's how you motivate your customers, and particularly your best customers, to continue doing business with you.

You must tell your story to those who aren't yet customers, in your content and in your marketing, to convey just how well you serve your customers and how you can solve your prospects' biggest problems. That's how you can attract more customers like the ones you serve now.

Here's the great news: Almost none of your competitors can do that.

Not one bit.

Not even close.

They don't survey their customers.

Those that might, do so badly.

Even those who collect *decent* data from their customers typically don't know how to use it.

That's why you can win. You can dominate . . . You can take the lead and stay there.

Phase III of Concierge Customer Service: Keeping the Gold Coming

Once you have your Concierge Customer Service system in place, it's imperative that you keep the customer feedback coming: Because customer sentiment changes, you must ensure that you constantly understand your customers' priorities, with the Opportunity Generator, and use the Feedback Generator to measure their satisfaction. Doing so will ensure that you consistently know your customers well, so you can serve them well.

And because you created and implemented the tools to do that in Phase I, Phase III allows you to leverage your investment. You will use the surveys you created in Phase I, on an ongoing basis—in fact, it's imperative that you do so, so that you have consistent measures that allow you to compare how customer sentiment, and that of your team, changes over time. If you change the measures, you lose that all-important comparability.

Keeping the data coming actually proves very easy. Once your surveys are created, you can set up a series of invitations in your CRM that you can send at designated intervals. Here are the steps:

- Step 1. Copy each of the Phase I surveys, so that your Time 2 data remain separate from the Time 1 (Phase I) data.
- Step 2. Set up your autoresponder to send out survey invitations at a designated interval. We generally recommend that you invite all of the customers who were invited to respond in Phase I 9-12 months after the Phase I survey.
- Step 3. Create another copy of the survey that will be used exclusively for new customers.
- Step 4. Create an autoresponder invitation series for new customers, modeled on the one you used for existing customers.
- Step 5. Survey new customers within 3 months after they become customers. Then feed them into the next survey cycle of the customer base.
- Step 6. Keep surveying your customers every 9-12 months.
- Step 7. Keep surveying your team every 9-12 months.

Notice several things about this system.
- First, it is a *system* that keeps feedback coming consistently.
- Second, because you're using the same instruments, you can track changes in sentiment over time, so you know if something changes that you need to attend to.
- Third, you're not spending $20,000 hiring a consultant to do your "annual survey," you're leveraging your Phase I investment.

- Fourth, you're not pestering your customers with a survey every quarter, or every month, or every week.
- Fifth, your feedback system pays for itself, because it will bolster retention and conversion. The added benefit will be testimonials and statistical data that can transform your marketing and content creation to skyrocket conversions further.

We recommend you either create separate surveys for the customers who do and who do not qualify for Concierge Customer Service or that you tag the responses, so that you can understand the preferences of each segment and how they may vary.

Mining Your Gold

Now that your system is created to gather current and useful customer and team feedback consistently, you have to mine your gold. Let's break it down so that you know exactly how to understand and put to work the information you'll collect.

Step 1: Response

The first step is to understand how well you secured response from the group to whom you sent survey invitations. Let's focus on your customer survey. As we indicated in Chapter 4, the larger the proportion of customers from whom you hear, the more *representative* your data will be—the more accurately the data will represent the characteristics and views of your customer base.

As part of this process, you should review:

- How many people opened each survey invitation? Hopefully, you have been reviewing your open rates throughout the survey. Now it's time to review the overall open rate. Note also the deliverability of your invitations (e.g., how many invitations reached the email address, as opposed to "bouncing").
- How many people clicked one of the survey links? This proves to be an important statistic to watch. Many online survey programs base *termination rates* (the proportion of individuals who begin the survey but do not complete it) upon the number of people who actually begin the survey. You'll typically find, though, that some individuals click the survey link without ever beginning the survey. That's why it's important to use click rates to track how many people you sent to the survey.
- How many people began the survey?
- How many people completed the survey?
- From this, calculate how many people terminated and the termination (or completion) rate.
- At what points in the survey did terminations occur— was there a particular question at which many respondents terminated? (Many survey software programs offer "fall off" reports that provide good detail on terminations.)
- Another important statistic is the response rate, which represents the proportion of the population (your customer base) that responded. When telephone surveys were the norm, we typically calculated response rates as the proportion of screened eligible respondents who completed the

survey—in other words, we divided the number of people who completed the survey by the number of people who (a) answered the phone, (b) completed any "screener" questions to determine eligibility, and (c) were deemed eligible. Organizations such as the American Association for Public Opinion Research (AAPOR) still focus on response rates in this way.

- o But for an online survey—which is what we strongly recommend for wholesale distribution companies—determining the appropriate denominator proves less clear.
- o I tend to recommend two different methods.
- o The first is to calculate the proportion of individuals who opened the email who then completed the survey. In that case, then, the denominator is the number of opens. This arguably provides the closest analogue to the proportion of screened eligible respondents.
- o The other way to calculate the response rate—which is more common—is to divide the number of completes by the number of delivered emails.

Step II: What Does Your Opportunity Generator Tell You?

To identify the top priorities and challenges of your customers, or "what keeps your customers awake at night," your Opportunity Generator question should show you what percentage of respondents find each of a series of issues highest priority; high but not highest; somewhat of a priority; or not a priority at all. The clearest way to interpret

the data is to simply (a) sum the percentage who rate each
issue EITHER highest priority OR high but not highest, then
(b) rank the issues on that total. Now you can see, clearly
and definitively, the top priorities of your customers.[18]

As you look at these data, sit back and think for a
minute. Some of this information probably confirms your
expectations. But it's highly likely that you also find some
surprises in there—we've never delivered Opportunity
Generator data to a client without delivering surprises.
Consider these questions:

- What story do the data tell you about the problems
  your customers face? How can you augment the
  quantitative data with qualitative detail?
- How might you make subtle changes to the way in
  which you interact with your customers, based upon
  this information?
- What additional services might you offer to help your
  customers deal with identified challenges or achieve
  their goals?
- What surprises you about the results and what
  confirms your expectations?

As we showed you in Chapter 4, this information
should inform how you orient Concierge Customer Service;
every single CCSR and CSR, and every single salesperson,
should know what these priorities are. This information also
proves invaluable for orienting your marketing and content
marketing—so you should share it with your marketing
team.

---

[18] We provide an example of Opportunity Generator data in Chapter 4.

Step III: Other Types of Opportunity Generator Data

Note also additional preferences regarding such key items as

- the customers' top choice for contacting a CSR or CCSR,
- how quickly they expect a response and/or quote from a CSR or CCSR, and
- what kinds of functions they would like to conduct online (e.g., checking invoices, paying bills, tracking deliveries, etc.).

Here, focus on how prevalent particular preferences are. Look also to see if certain types of customers have different preferences, on average, than other types of customers do.

Step IV: What Does Your Feedback Generator Tell You?

Your Feedback Generator data provide a wealth of information on both the areas in which you excel and your opportunities for improvement. You should craft a specific list of areas that fall into each of these two categories—so you compile a list of (a) accomplishments to celebrate and (b) areas on which to focus, to ensure continuous process improvement.

But how do you decide which results indicate an area of improvement, as opposed to an area in which you excel? We can provide some simple guidelines. Most of the scales in your feedback generator will typically be 4-point satisfaction scales (very satisfied, somewhat satisfied, somewhat dissatisfied, very dissatisfied).[19] To understand these data, look at them in two ways. First, sum (a) the percentage of respondents who are satisfied with the percentage who are very satisfied and (b) the percentage who are very dissatisfied with the percentage who are somewhat dissatisfied. Your goal should be to achieve at least 90% total satisfaction on both the general and specific satisfaction measures. Those are the areas in which you can celebrate your achievements, both internally and in your marketing. Where the scores fall below that 90% threshold, you've identified opportunities for improvement on which you should work with your team.

Look also at the percentage of respondents who fall in the "top box" (e.g., the percentage who are "very satisfied," as opposed to "somewhat satisfied"). Particularly for items related to customer service, order delivery, and other key issues, you should strive to see at least 75% of respondents in the "very satisfied" category. Remember, your Phase I data will be used as a baseline against which to compare each successive data wave.

Step V: What Do Your Open-Ended Responses Tell You?

Ideally, your survey should rely mostly on closed-ended questions, because these are the easiest for your customers to answer and also the easiest to analyze. But

---

[19] Notice that we did not include a neutral category. A large literature deals with the issue of whether to include or exclude a neutral category. Although a case can be made for either position, we believe that in a business context, it's advantageous to exclude the neutral category so that the "fence sitters" or "floaters" have to choose one end of the scale or the other, as this provides more direction for the business.

it's good to include a few open-ended questions (we recommend about 80% closed-ended and 20% open-ended) to (a) pick up on the nuances and meaning that closed-ended questions miss, (b) to get the "language" your customers are using, and (c) to identify some things you might not have captured with your closed-ended categories. Remember, though, that you should not simply read through the open-ended questions, because your brain can mislead you about what you see. "Code" the responses by identifying the key categories or themes and summarize, in a spreadsheet, how many respondents mention those themes.

Leveraging the Gold You've Mined

Once you have this system in place, it will help you ensure that you provide Concierge Customer Service to your most profitable customers and good service to everyone. But remember that these data also provide gold for your marketing—if you use the data effectively.

Testimonials should definitely appear prominently on your website—on your homepage, on a separate testimonials page, and/or in a sidebar on EVERY page of your website, so your customers and prospective customers find this social proof at every turn. Add testimonials to your product and/or service pages and include them in pages on which you have a call to action (CTA). Add to your "contact us" page testimonials that highlight your wonderful customer service. Incorporate them into your blog and on your Facebook and LinkedIn pages; add them to social media ads and posts, as well. Weave testimonials into your case studies, to enliven them and to augment *your* descriptions of your customers' transformation with comments in the customer's own words. Include them in email marketing campaigns and print marketing materials.

And don't forget to share glowing testimonials with your team, to boost morale and celebrate accomplishments.

Satisfaction Data should also be used throughout your marketing assets and campaigns. Suppose you find that 95% of your customers are satisfied and 98% would recommend your business. Don't keep those facts secret! As with testimonials, these data should go everywhere—and often, they should be used in tandem with your testimonials. By combining or juxtaposing testimonials with statistical data, you gain the ability to appeal to prospects' and customers' logic AND to their emotions.

Here's an example of that principle in action. A Louisiana insurance company was doing battle with one of our local hospitals over contract terms a few years ago. The insurance company launched two 30-second ads that ran back-to-back. In the first, a woman recounted the heart-rending story of how her daughter faced a life-threatening illness and how the insurance company covered all the costs of the care that saved her daughter's life. On the heels of that spot came an ad that posed the question, "Did you know that $.52 of every dollar we pay to this hospital goes to something OTHER than patient care?" The first spot targeted emotions and the second aimed at logic. The power of this is reflected in the fact that I still remember that commercial, years later.

As with testimonials, your satisfaction data should appear throughout your website. They should be woven into your content marketing, print marketing materials, product pages, contact us page, and every call to action. Use them liberally throughout social media posts, ads, and pages. And, as with your testimonials, ensure that you share these data with your team.

How to Avoid Common Data Pitfalls

As you can see by now, the data you collect stand at the core of creating content people will consume, products they long to buy, and marketing messages that convert. It really is the "holy grail." What's shocking to me is how few businesses have a system with which to gather the data they need and use them in the ways we just outlined. When I first left academia to strike out on my own as a consultant, I didn't understand that—and I really didn't think I had much to offer businesses. I assumed that they were already getting the data they needed and using it effectively. Well, as the old adage says, the consequences when we "assume" aren't good: I found out quickly that many, perhaps MOST businesses weren't getting the data they needed or using them well. What's more, most businesses who face these problems don't even realize what they lack or how high the costs of inaction are—they "don't know what they don't know." This is why survey design and data analysis are so important.

Here are some questions to ask yourself about YOUR business, right now:

1. *Are you drowning in data?* "Big data" can bring both costs and benefits: Avanade (2017) reports that 62% of C-level executives complain of interruptions from "irrelevant data." But executives also complain that they *lack* the data they need to make key

decisions. Ensure that you gather and use the data you need to implement and maintain your Concierge Customer Service system and then use it effectively.

2. ***Do you have a SYSTEM for gathering customer feedback that also generates social proof?*** No matter how well you understand the importance of gathering customer feedback and social proof, unless you build and maintain a *system* for gathering and leveraging these data, you're missing huge opportunities. I consulted once with a $100-million consulting company that did corporate turnarounds. Because they took companies from the brink of bankruptcy to profitability, they should have offered hundreds of glowing testimonials and dozens of case studies on their website. But they had virtually none. The reason? No system—and no system means no data and no results. One of the key benefits of your Concierge Customer Service System is that gathering social proof is a natural byproduct of implementing your system.

3. ***Are you using your customer data effectively?*** Once you collect information from your customers through surveys, you can bring that information into your CRM to "tag" attitudes, behaviors, and preferences. Having information in your CRM on, for example, how given customers prefer to order, how fast they expect response, and demographic characteristics of the individuals with whom you deal can prove extraordinarily useful by allowing you to tailor your customer service to individual preferences and also target particular types of communication at

particular types of customers. Obviously, one of the most basic forms of list segmentation will be segmenting the customers who are eligible for Concierge Customer Service from those who do not qualify.

4. ***Are you enriching your customer data?*** Data appends, in which you "enrich" your data by appending demographic, firmographic, industry, and even social media information, provide a powerful, cost-effective tool that far too many wholesale distribution companies fail to leverage. This can provide invaluable information on the companies with whom you work and with whom you would like to work, as well as the individuals who make decisions or serve as points of contact in those companies.

Your "Unfair" Advantage

Once you put your system in place to keep data coming in and use them effectively, you should see tremendous changes in your ability to convert and captivate customers. The simple but powerful techniques we've provided in this chapter can and will produce tremendous profitability gains by ensuring that you know and serve your customers well, day after day and year after year. But it's never a "one size fits all" model. In the next chapter, we offer information to help you understand how attracting and serving Millennials differs from the way in which you attract and serve members of other generations.

"The more you engage with customers, the clearer things become and the easier it is to determine what you should be doing." – John Russell

CHAPTER 7: Adapting Your CCS System to Different Generations

We hear the stereotypes every day: "Millennials are entitled—they just don't want to work the way our generation did." "We have less opportunity than our parents did because the Baby Boomers won't retire." Or "Millennials have been unfairly maligned—if managers could work with us more effectively, we'd all become more productive."

These statements reflect the impact of differences among generational *cohorts*—some real, some perceived. Demographers (scientists who study population) use the term "cohort" to describe a group of people born in a particular time period. And, although some of the differences among cohorts can be vastly overstated and "individual results vary," there's no question that certain characteristics are more prevalent in some cohorts than in others.

In this chapter, we provide information on the major generational cohorts in the United States. Understanding the differences among cohorts plays an important role in the implementation of your Concierge Customer Service system, in two ways. First, the more you understand cohort differences in orientations and expectations, the better you can tailor your service. Second, because ensuring employee engagement and satisfaction proves so important to customer satisfaction, understanding how cohort differences come into play can help you improve all of those outcomes. And, as you work to attract customers like those you serve already, understanding these generational differences will let you tailor your marketing to these different cohorts.[20] Before we dig into the data on cohorts, let's look at the structure of generational cohorts and at some of the general patterns in age differences that are relevant.

Generational Differences in Internet and Social Media Use

It probably doesn't surprise you to learn that the percentage of adults who use the Internet and social media sites has risen precipitously over the last decade. Pew Research, who has tracked these trends since 2000, reports that 52% of Americans used the Internet in 2000; by 2016, 88% reported Internet use (Pew Research Center, 2017a).

If we focus specifically on social media use, the rise has been more recent and more dramatic: Whereas only 5% of American adults reported social media use in 2005 (when Pew Research Center began tracking that statistic), that number soared to 69% of the American adult population by 2016 (Pew Research Center, 2017b). The fact that more than 2 out of 3 American adults use social media underscores the importance of using content marketing to connect with customers and prospective customers in social

---

[20] There are numerous sources on which to draw for this information. We've relied heavily on Pew Research Center because the data they use are reliable (they come Pew's research and from government sources and are analyzed well) but also are accessible and easily understood. On the Pew website (www.PewResearch.org), you can access much of the data that underlie the charts we've included, if you're interested in getting more information.

media, as well as the need to use the Opportunity Generator to understand what kind of content your market wants to consume.

Figure 7.1

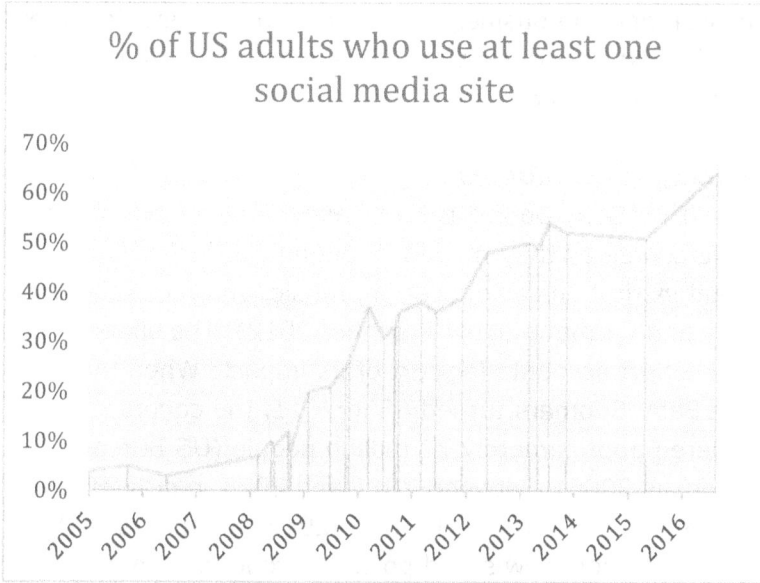

% of US adults who use at least one social media site

If the data on internet and social media use don't surprise you, the age distribution of social media use might. Whereas a scant 3% of Americans over age 65 used at least one social media site in 2005, 34% reported social media use in 2016 (Pew Research Center, 2017b). Granted, the level of social media use among younger cohorts dwarfs that statistic (86% of Americans between 18 and 29 used at least one site, as did 80% of those between 30 and 49 and 64% of 50-64 year olds (Pew Research Center 2017b)). But the fact that more than 1 in 3 Americans over 65 uses social media reminds us of how strongly social media has permeated the American landscape, even among older Americans.[21] If rates stand this high in the general population, we can safely assume that the rates stand even higher among the businesspeople in your market. Now that we've looked at some key age differences, let's understand the characteristics of 3 key cohorts.

The Baby Boom Cohort

The "Baby Boom" cohort has redefined each stage of the life course as they moved through it, affecting such societal institutions as education, music, and race relations (Colby and Ortman, 2014; Pruchno, 2012). The sheer size of the cohort accounts for part of its impact: When the first of the Baby Boomers turned 65 in 2011, the cohort numbered approximately 77 million people (US Bureau of the Census 2006). Between 2011 and 2028, nearly 10,000 people a day will turn 65 (Pruchno 2012). Members of this enormous cohort now stand poised to redefine American conceptions and norms regarding aging, health, and retirement. Because they are active, adept, influential, and control a substantial portion of wealth in the United States, they attract considerable attention. And, because they are likely to remain a presence in the American workforce for years to come, understanding them becomes important for both customer service and marketing efforts.

---

[21] Fully 36% of those over 65 report using Facebook, whereas only 11% use LinkedIn.

Who Are the Baby Boomers and Why Do They Matter to Your Business?

The term "Baby Boomers" refers to the cohort born in the United States between the middle of 1946 (just after World War II, when birth rates rose sharply) and the middle of 1964, when birth rates fell (Hogan, Perez, & Bell, 2008).[22] Because birth years in this cohort span 19 years, some analysts distinguish between the "leading edge" or "early" Boomers (individuals born between 1946 and 1955) and the "trailing edge" or "late" Boomers (born between 1956 and 1964).

Here are some key facts of which your salespeople and customer service representatives should remain cognizant when dealing with Baby Boomers:

1. ***They don't "feel old."*** Baby Boomers don't believe that old age begins until age 72; 61% of Baby Boomers report that they "feel younger"—9 years younger, in fact—than their chronological age (Pew Research 2009). That statistic carries a caution for those who serve and who craft messages for this generation: Because they don't "feel old" and because they so strongly want to remain active, vital, and productive, customer service, sales, and marketing messages should align with these sentiments.

---

[22] We note that such other countries as France, the United Kingdom, Canada, Finland, The Netherlands, New Zealand, and Australia experienced a post-war Baby Boom around the same time; Germany's boom came somewhat later. Russia experienced a decline, rather than an increase in post-war birth rates because the war decimated the male population of reproductive ages.

2. ***Baby Boomers are Increasingly Tech Savvy.***
   Although younger cohorts (i.e., Generation X and the
   Millennials) are more likely than Baby Boomers to
   use social networking sites, Baby Boomers' social
   network usage has increased dramatically in recent
   years. Social media use among older Boomers (50-
   64) increased from 4% in 2005 to 64% in 2016 (Pew
   Research Center 2017b). *This means that even when
   decision-makers in the companies with whom you
   deal are part of this cohort, you still need to ensure
   that you're using social media to attract and serve
   them.* At the same time, you must remember that
   there is probably more diversity in technological
   knowledge and usage in this cohort than in any
   other. For that reason, ensuring that you understand
   individual preferences and patterns regarding
   communication and ordering becomes particularly
   important for customers who are Boomers.

3. ***Boomers May Not Retire As Early As Their
   Parents and Grandparents Did.*** By 2016, the US
   had over 9.2 million people over 65 in the civilian
   labor force; more than 1.7 million were over age 75.
   That trend is predicted to continue, so that by 2024
   workers over the age of 65 are projected to account
   for 6.1% of the total labor force; by 2022, we are
   projected to have more than 13 million individuals
   over 65 and 2.8 million over 75 in the civilian labor
   force (Bureau of Labor Statistics 2017). And since
   1995, the percentage of older workers employed full
   time, rather than part time, has increased. Factors
   causing Boomers to remain in the labor force longer

include changes in Social Security; increased use of defined contribution (as opposed to defined benefit) pension plans, such as 401(k)s; the fact that individuals are largely remaining healthier in their later years; and the fact that some individuals may not have enough savings to retire early. Opinion polls support these data: Only about one-quarter (27%) of Baby Boomers say they expect to retire before age 65, about another quarter (24%) say they plan to retire at 65. But nearly 4 in 10 (39%) plan to work until they are 66 or older and fully 10% say they will "never" retire (Harter and Agrawal, 2014). This means that your salespeople and customer service representatives are likely to continue serving members of the Baby Boom cohort for many years. When we consider the statistics above regarding rates of Internet and social media use among those over 65, it becomes clear that content marketing will remain important even for older customers.

Generation X

The first cohort that followed the Baby Boom was born between about 1965 and 1980. Once referred to as the "Baby Bust," reflecting the sharp decline in birth rates after about 1964, it was later dubbed "Generation X." In many of their attitudes and behaviors, Generation X stands "in the middle," between the Baby Boom cohort that precedes it and the Millennial cohort that follows. Although the "Baby Boom" cohort has been defined clearly and described, the cohorts that came after it—whose lines of demarcation are more blurred—often receive less attention. One important characteristic of this cohort is that Generation X can be seen as the demographic "bridge" to US diversity: Whereas the Baby Boom population is over 70% non-Hispanic white, that statistic falls to 61% among Generation X and 57% among the Millennials (Pew Research 2014). By 2000, 1 in 6 members of the Generation X cohort was a foreign-born immigrant (Carlson 2009).

Communication Platforms

On several measures of online and social media use, Generation X members lie "in the middle" between the lower adoption rates of Baby Boomers and the higher rates among Millennials; this includes the percentage who have shared a "selfie" on social media and the median number of Facebook friends (Pew Research Center 2017b). Despite these trends, Generation Xers still have a strong online presence. In fact, Pew Research reported in 2009 that 80% of Generation X members shopped online and that they were the cohort most likely to engage in online banking (67%). More recent data show that, as of 2015, 64% of Americans between the ages of 30 and 49 reported that they would buy something online via cell phone and 19% (nearly 1 in 5) would do so with a social media link (Pew Research Center 2017b). Because we see these consumer behavior patterns increasingly reflected in buying preferences of our wholesale distribution clients' customers, we think it is important to consider these patterns as you craft your ecommerce strategy. Given this high online presence and connection to others through social media, businesses serving and marketing to decision makers in

Generation X would also be wise to do such things as offering testimonials on their websites, to increase their visibility and grab the attention of Generation X.

The vast majority (over 90%) of Generation X members own cell phones. Given these high rates of cell phone activity, communication, customer service and marketing strategies aimed at Generation X should include mobile strategies—this means, for example, that websites must have responsive design and marketing campaigns should include mobile strategies. The mantra is no longer "mobile friendly" but now "mobile first."

It is also important to note that, because members of Generation X are so strongly connected to social media, they have the potential to affect others' opinions and actions: They can either promote a business, by serving as a brand advocate and "referral generator," or harm a business by posting harmful content about its products and services. This underscores the importance of keeping your finger on the pulse of customer sentiment, to ensure that the messages they disseminate remain positive. As you develop strategies for attracting, communicating with, and serving customers in this cohort, it is also important to ensure that communication through these media rests on a focused strategy.

Demographic, Educational, and Economic Characteristics

Members of this cohort are more educated than their Baby Boom predecessors: Whereas the majority (54%) of Baby Boomers held a high school diploma or less at age 25-32, only 46% of Generation X members reported that level of educational attainment (Taylor and Gao 2014). Generation X is the first generation in which more women than men graduated college (US Bureau of the Census 2006; Carlson 2009). Data also show that they have delayed marriage and childbearing more than their predecessors; demographers attribute this to the fact that women were completing education and beginning careers, while men often faced employment challenges (Carlson 2009).

Economic demographer David Foot describes Generation X as a cohort that became nimble out of necessity: They often shifted, and continue to shift, across jobs, occupations, and industries. Population Reference Bureau analysts echo that description for Generation X *men* in the US, noting considerable unemployment and slow career advancement. Women, however, have entered paid employment more quickly than their Baby Boom counterparts (Carlson 2009).

The occupational challenges of this cohort are reflected in earnings among Generation X men: In real dollars, men in this cohort earned 12% less than their fathers earned in 1974, at the same age. They were the first generation of males in the US in this century to have that experience. The high employment rates of women in Generation X became important for household wellbeing (US Bureau of the Census 2006).

Why do these data matter for you, as you craft customer service and marketing messages for this cohort? Because these statistics suggest that members of Generation X are less trusting and more cynical about social institutions than their predecessors are (although not as lacking in trust as Millennials). Decision makers in this cohort may be particularly likely to need social proof (testimonials, statistical data, and/or case studies) before making a purchase. In short, you, your customer service personnel, and your salespeople will likely have to work much harder to win the trust of this generation than you did to engage their predecessors.

Political and Social Views

According to General Social Survey (GSS) data, individuals in Generation X are more likely than any generation before them to describe themselves as politically independent and to eschew political party identification (Carlson 2009). As with many other characteristics, their political views tend to fall between the more conservative beliefs of the Baby Boom and the more liberal attitudes of the Millennials. They are more likely than the Baby Boomers and less likely than Millennials to say they want a bigger government with more services and to favor allowing gays and lesbians to marry; they are less likely than Baby Boomers and more likely than Millennials to say that unauthorized immigrants should not be allowed to stay in the country legally and to say that "a patriotic person" describes them well. Companies who serve and market to Generation X need to understand these patterns, which clearly distinguish this cohort from the Baby Boomers.

Millennials

This cohort, which follows Generation X, has been defined as those born between 1981 and 1997 (Fry 2016). Like the Boomer cohort, the sheer size of the Millennial cohort presents major opportunities for your business—but capitalizing upon those opportunities also requires that you understand how to attract Millennials and serve them effectively.

Who Are the Millennials?

Two characteristics of Millennials prove particularly relevant for the businesses who deal with them. First, members of the Millennial cohort are, by far, more "connected" online than either the Baby Boom or Generation X cohorts that precede them. Millennials participate strongly in social media (Pew Research Center (2017b) reports that over 85% use social media), the Internet, and mobile technologies; online social networks provide a key focus of their interaction. Millennials' online behavior reflects the fact that this is the first generation to grow up with these technologies. Because this cohort is the most internet-savvy, Millennials are likely to do their research (e.g., searching for a comparable rate, better service, and reading reviews) before making a purchase. The second salient characteristic is that, as we noted in Chapter 1, Millennials' level of trust stands lower than that of any other cohort in the workforce.

Here are some of the implications of those two characteristics:

1. When we consider together the technological savvy of Millennials and their low levels of trust, this suggests that you must ensure you not only communicate your message well online but also that you provide the "social proof" —in the form of testimonials, statistical data, and/or case studies—

that Millennials look for. Once you have completed Phases I, II, and III of putting your Concierge Customer Service system in place, you should have a steady flow of all of these forms of social proof. Then you need to use them effectively and widely, as we outline in Chapter 6.

2. Because Millennials often want to "do it their way," technologically, your ecommerce, website, and ordering technologies must remain up to date and you must understand your customers' preferences well. For example, many of the wholesale distribution clients with whom we work find that Millennials often want to text orders in, rather than submitting online or by phone. This is one reason that "tagging" information to segment customers in your CRM is so important. This enables your salespeople and customer service representatives to know customers' preferences easily.

3. Because Millennials are strongly connected to social media, they have the potential to affect others' opinions and actions, either positively or negatively. *It is important to remember, then, that excellent product or service quality, as well as customer service, prove particularly important for this generation.*

4. Ask yourself these questions:

   a. Are you putting out content marketing that focuses on issues that you *know* Millennial decision makers care about?

   b. Are you leveraging social media effectively?

    c. Are you ensuring that your customer list is segmented by generation?

    d. Are you targeting your marketing messages correctly for Millennials?

    e. Are you maintaining a strong, optimized web presence?

    f. Is your website clean and clear, offering good functionality? Remember, many Millennials built websites in school!

    g. Are you providing customer service that differentiates your company?

Education and Employment

Millennials stand poised to become the best-educated cohort in American history. Roughly 21% of men in this cohort hold a bachelor's degree and 27% of women do (Patten and Fry 2015). This trend reflects the steady increase in the proportion of individuals with college degrees in the US, more broadly, over the last few decades. Because many Millennials have been unable to find jobs after completing their undergraduate studies, many have pursued advanced degrees. In part because of job challenges, Millennial-headed households are more likely than households headed by members of any other generational cohort to live in poverty (Fry 2017b). Although many argue that Millennials are more prone to "job hop" than their predecessors, Pew Research's analysis of data from the US Department of Labor[23] revealed that Millennials between the ages of 18 and 35 prove to be just as likely to

---

[23] The data came from the Current Population Survey.

remain with an employer as members of Generation X were, at a similar age (Fry 2017a).[24] The higher level of education among Millennials means that they are likely to be discerning and analytical. Both your salespeople and your customer services representatives must, therefore, understand and respond appropriately to that fact. The higher level of education among Millennials also presents an opportunity to develop content and marketing strategies that are both stimulating and thought-provoking.

What do They Value?

To attract and serve Millennials, your salespeople and customer service representatives need to understand who Millennials are and what they value. Here are their top values, according to Pew Research Center:

1. *Family*. When Pew Research Center asked Millennials to identity their top priorities, one theme emerged— family. Millennials reported that (1) being a good parent and (2) having a successful marriage stand among their top priorities; correspondingly, they are less likely than older cohorts to "trade off" family priorities for career success. But their definition of family often differs from that of previous cohorts, as they are more likely to embrace single-parent and/or multi-racial or multi-ethnic family structures than older generations are. Millennials comprise about ½ of cohabiting households in the US and have more

---

[24] In fact, Millennials who hold college degrees remain with their employers longer, on average, than members of the Generation X cohort did at the same age. These findings suggest that the employment pattern among Millennials represents a maturation, rather than a cohort effect (please see the discussion, at the end of this chapter, of those two types of effects).

households headed by single mothers than any other generational cohort (Fry 2017b). In 2016, they became the cohort with the largest number of household heads who identified themselves as multi-racial (Fry 2017b).

2. *Diversity*. The most ethnically diverse American generation ever, the Millennial cohort is 43% non-white,[25] with that diversity fueled in part by Hispanic and Asian immigration. According to the Pew Research Center, this diversity has led to higher levels of racial tolerance than has been seen in the cohorts of their predecessors.

3. *Independence*. Perhaps one of the most commented-upon characteristics of the Millennials is their lack of connection to key social institutions. Compared to previous generations, they demonstrate lower levels of religious affiliation (nearly 3 in 10 are unaffiliated with a religion) and are more likely to define themselves as politically independent (50% identify as independents).

---

[25] We note that the US Bureau of the Census projections estimate that the US population will become majority non-white by 2043.

Generational Trends

In 2015, the Millennial cohort became the largest living generation, eclipsing the Baby Boomers (Fry 2016). And, as we noted in Chapter 1, they comprise the largest generational segment of the workforce (United States Bureau of the Census 2006). Projections estimate that the size of the Millennial cohort will peak in 2036, at 81.1 million members (Fry 2016). Census bureau projections predict that, by 2028, Generation X will also exceed the Baby Boom generation in size. The size of this cohort is predicted to reach its apex in 2018, at 65.8 million members.

Figure 7.2

Projected population by generation

In millions

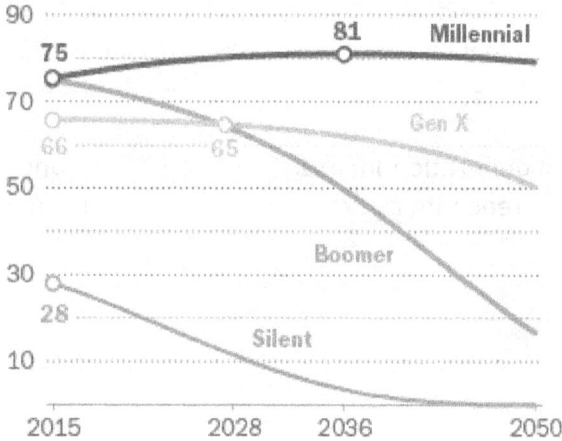

Note: Millennials refers to the population ages 18 to 34
as of 2015.
Source: Pew Research Center tabulations of U.S. Census
Bureau population projections released December 2014 and
2015 population estimates

PEW RESEARCH CENTER

Implications and Limitations

Understanding generational differences is key for
your personnel—particularly sales representatives, customer
service representatives, and Concierge Customer Service
Representatives—as part of your mission to "know your
customers well so you can serve them well." Yet despite the

importance and utility of these data, we note that substantial variation across individuals, within cohorts, exists.

We also note that it's sometimes difficult to separate the kind *cohort effects* that we've described here from *maturation effects.* Here's what we mean by that: When we look at generational differences at a given point in time (using what we call *cross-sectional data*, or data from a single time point), we can't discern to what extent differences between an older group of workers and a younger group of workers exist because of the period in which these individuals were born and reared, or simply because of changes that happen as people move through the life course. Here's an example. Let's suppose you collect data from your employees and see that your Millennial employees have lower satisfaction than either members of the "Generation X" cohort or the Baby Boomers in your employ. Your first instinct might be to adopt the "Millennials are different/entitled/impossible to satisfy" argument. If you're right, this means that the differences owe to the different circumstances in which Millennials were reared—so the pattern is primarily a *cohort effect*. However, research shows that job satisfaction tends to change, in predictable ways, as individuals move through the life course—it tends to increase up until mid-career, then decline somewhat. Those effects represent *maturation*, rather than *cohort* effects. The question becomes, then, will Millennials' job satisfaction remain low or will it follow the pattern of earlier generations? Time will tell.

Adopting a Generational Perspective

Your success depends increasingly upon adapting to the different values and preferences of these generational cohorts. These differences affect the internal dynamics in your company, the strategies you use to attract and convert prospects of different ages, the kind of service you must offer to different customers, and the kinds of ecommerce and website options you provide. In the next chapter, we provide some action items to consider, for this chapter and for those that preceded it.

"You'll never have a product or a price advantage again. They can be easily duplicated, but a strong customer service culture can't be copied." – Jerry Fritz

CHAPTER 8: Know Them Well and Serve Them Well

Now you have it. The framework of this system. You have the blueprint of a Concierge Customer Service System and you see how they fit together. You see the benefits and I hope you also understand the *necessity* of putting this system in place, of pursuing customer-centric innovation. In this chapter, we're going to review the components and derive a series of action steps for you, referencing the chapters as we do so that you can return easily to material you want to review.

Why Bother? We began, in Chapter 1, by placing the concept and principles of Concierge Customer Service within the context of the disruptive changes that wholesale distributors face right now. But we also placed it in the context of broader social dynamics, using sociological theory to show *why* these changes are happening. We drew upon Max Weber's organizational analysis to show you how you can use the principles of *specialization* and *division of labor* to navigate successfully the changes you face, through implementation of Concierge Customer Service. We outlined the core benefits of doing so, which include but are not limited to **Conversion**, **Penetration** of your market, and **Retention** of your customers—particularly your most profitable customers. CCS can also increase your lead flow, ensure continuous process improvement, provide customer service bellwethers, and yield benefits for your personnel.

The key **action items** from that chapter are:

1. Outline the current market disruptions and threats that you face;
2. Review the list of indicators of disruption that we offered in Chapter 1 and see how many represent your experience:
    a. Are you feeling margin pressure?
    b. Are your personnel costs escalating?
    c. Are your best customers defecting to competitors whom you *know* aren't as good as your company is?
    d. Does your business model seem less relevant to the market than it was 10-20 years ago?
    e. Does your company lack flexibility or budget to do the things it used to do?

Your answers to these questions assist you AND your team to identify key motivations to change. Bottom line, you enjoy an opportunity to retain your best, most profitable customers by providing Concierge Customer Service to them and, in so doing, capture more customers *like* them. That lets you capitalize upon two of the key benefits of bureaucracy—*specialization* and *division of labor*—while avoiding the bureaucratic inefficiencies that conspire to create an "iron cage" for both your customers and your employees.

Adopting The CCS Mindset. In Chapter 2, we illustrated how reaping the benefits of specialization and division of labor, through the CCS system, provides benefits for both your customers *and* your employees. We provided research demonstrating that keeping your *customers* satisfied requires that you also keep your *employees* satisfied, which is why we covered both topics. Then, we outlined the 4 principles of the CCS system, which include giving customers MORE—ensuring that your employees maintain the right *mindset,* that they take *ownership* of customers' problems, that they create *referability* by doing so, and ensure an exceptional customer *experience*. And we showed you that research demonstrates clearly the benefits that flow to your bottom line when you ensure that both your customers and your employees are happy, producing as much as fourfold increases in revenue growth through gains in employee retention and customer satisfaction.

Action items for that chapter include:

1. Review recent data on customer satisfaction and engagement—and if you don't have those data, consider why;
2. Review recent data on employee satisfaction and engagement—and if you don't have those data, consider why;
3. Consider carefully if and how your customer service system embodies the 4 key principles of mindset, taking ownership of problems, making your company referable, and providing a superior customer experience.

We'll build upon these action items in the action items for Chapter 4, which outlined Phase I of instituting Concierge Customer Service.

How to Afford CCS. Because implementing Concierge Customer Service requires both commitment and investment, Chapter 3 outlined the financial foundations. The key to structuring your system to increase profitability lies in using profit analytics to identify the minority of customers who likely generate virtually *all* of your gross profit. You can then offer CCS to the top 10-15% of your customers who generate the greatest profit, typically because their cost to serve stands lower than that of other accounts. This ensures that you can retain your most profitable customers by providing a level of service that your competitors can't match.

Key ***action items*** regarding the financial foundations of CCS are:

1. Do you have profit analytics in place so you understand which customers generate profit and on which customers you actually lose money?
2. If you do, review those data carefully to ensure you know who your most profitable customers are.
3. If you do not have profit analytics in place, consider adopting a system such as WayPoint Analytics.
4. Ensure that your profit analytics let you see the balance between operating cash and cost-to-serve dollars on every invoice, in every account, in every territory.
5. Make necessary preparations to eventually lose accounts who are hurting your bottom line.
6. Look carefully at your salespeople, to see how diverse their roles are. If you see that they currently must generate prospects, qualify leads, set appointments, make presentations, do follow-up

calls, provide customer service, and even bear responsibility for collecting accounts, consider how you can use specialization and division of labor to increase the efficiency of your salesforce.

Because you must tailor your Concierge Customer Service system to your organization, your team, and your customers—and following the dictum that you can't serve them well if you don't know them well—chapter 4 shows how **Phase I of Concierge Customer Service** entails understanding, from your customers' point of view, what kind of service they want and tailoring the service to their preferences. To do that, you collect data that tell you (a) what your customers want and (b) how satisfied they are with the extent to which you're giving them what they want, using the Opportunity Generator and the Feedback Generator. You then elicit input from your team, to understand their view of customers' satisfaction and customer service, as well as their satisfaction and engagement.

Key **action items** for Chapter 4 include addressing these questions:

1. Are you using surveys to gather general satisfaction data?
2. Are you using surveys to measure specific satisfaction with such things as customer service, the degree to which customer service representatives advocate for your customers, the extent to which customers perceive customer service representatives to be friendly and professional, and the customer's

ability to get to the right person immediately when a problem arises?

3. Are your surveys generating testimonials, with permission to use them?
4. Are you creating referrals through surveys?
5. Are you using surveys to generate online reviews?
6. Do you use best practices in your surveys, such as providing an incentive, making the surveys customer-centric, sending multiple invitations, and reporting back to customers and your team on the results?

To put **Concierge Customer Service** in place, you must first ensure that your team is on board, create a system, and train your employees carefully in that system. That's why, in Chapter 5, we suggest that you begin Phase II by presenting the results of your Phase I surveys to your team and then introducing the concept of Concierge Customer Service, all via webinar. Then you must identify customers who are eligible for CCS; specify the elements of your CCS system, including job descriptions and benefits; and put your system in place.

Key **action items** for Chapter 5 include:

1. Evaluating your current customer service;
2. Using profit analytics to identify customers who would be eligible for Concierge Customer Service;
3. Designing your Concierge Customer Service system;
4. Reviewing the results of your internal and customer surveys with your team, via webinar;
5. Introducing your CCS system to your team, via webinar;

6. Identifying candidates for CCS representatives;
7. Defining clearly your CCS representative job description;
8. Identifying and screening CCS representative candidates;
9. Designating and training your CCS representatives;
10. Clarifying the structure of your CCS system and identifying clearly the benefits for your customers (and, in that process, identifying who in your company (a) is responsible for ensuring delivery of those benefits and (b) is involved in delivering them);
11. Ensuring that all CCS representatives understand and implement your CCS process when they work with customers;
12. Instituting a system for tracking all customer complaints, enabling you to (a) report back to the customer at least quarterly on problems you solved for him or her and (b) track customer issues, so that you can intervene to reduce problems and complaints;
13. Introducing your CCS program to eligible customers;
14. Planning for retention, turnover, and succession in the critical CCS representative position, ensuring that evaluation and feedback systems are in place; and
15. Possibly instituting an internal customer service team.

Once you put your CCS system in place, you must ensure that it consistently serves your customers well.

Chapter 6 shows you how to do so by garnering constant feedback on customer sentiment. And then you must use those data effectively. The bad news is that doing that effectively isn't easy—but the good news is that you can now leverage your Phase I investment to keep customer feedback coming in. As it does, you need to ensure that those data don't land and remain in a silo, but instead are disseminated throughout your company, to all relevant stakeholders, to ensure continuous process improvement. And then you should garner additional benefits by leveraging these data in your marketing, so you share far and wide the story of how you know and serve your customers well. That's how you mine your gold.

Key *action items* for garnering these benefits include:

1. Building a system that allows you to (a) repeat the survey questions you asked of customers during Phase I, so you elicit feedback from them every 9-12 months and (b) ask these questions of new customers within 3 months of the inception of your relationship, then 9-12 months thereafter;
2. Building a similar system to survey your employees every 9-12 months;
3. Using your Opportunity Generator data effectively;
4. Using your Feedback Generator data effectively;
5. Leveraging your testimonials and satisfaction data in your marketing; and
6. Avoiding common data pitfalls.

Adapting to Generational Differences. Your Opportunity Generator and Feedback Generator provide information on your customers that proves vital in serving them, retaining them, and attracting more customers like them. But there's another source of data you need to understand, to make your Concierge Customer Service system, and your marketing, effective: data on generational cohorts. Understanding how the Baby Boomers resemble and differ from the Generation X and Millennial cohorts proves vital for your company and your employees. That's why Chapter 7 provides information on who these cohorts are and how you need to respond.

Key *action items* from this information include:

1. Even if many of the decision makers in the companies your serve come from the Baby Boom cohort, recognize that you must still use social media to attract and serve them.

2. Recognize, too, that great diversity in technological adoption exists in the Baby Boom cohort. That means you must know how individuals prefer to communicate and order.

3. Understand that, because many Baby Boomers plan to delay retirement, you will likely continue to serve Baby Boomers for many years to come. Because of the difference between this cohort and both Generational X and Millennials, recognizing and responding to generational differences will remain important.

4. Because of the extent to which Generation X and especially Millennials use mobile phones, you must design websites and marketing campaigns to be responsive. Your mantra must be "mobile first."

5. Recognize the high levels of social media use among Generation X and Millennials; customers who belong to these cohorts can and do affect others' opinions and actions. They can either promote a business, by serving as a brand advocate and "referral generator," or harm a business by posting harmful content about its products and services. This underscores the importance of keeping your finger on the pulse of customer sentiment, to ensure that the messages they disseminate remain positive.

6. Members of Generation X and especially members of the Millennial cohort prove to be less trusting and more cynical about social institutions than their predecessors are. That makes it imperative to ensure that you provide social proof to support their decisions.

7. Because Millennials now comprise the largest generational segment of the US workforce (US Bureau of the Census), you must understand the Millennials. You must know how to manage them, as employees, and how to attract and serve them, as customers.

8. Leveraging the testimonials and statistical data that Phase III provides will prove increasingly important in attracting and serving Millennial customers.

9. As the proportion of Millennial decision makers in companies increases, expect that the demand for such things as the ability to text orders to your company will increase. This is one reason that "tagging" information to segment customers in your CRM becomes critical, so that your salespeople and

customer service representatives can know
customers' preferences easily.

Making It Count

Now you have the information you need to put your
Concierge Customer Service system in place and ensure
that you know your customers so well that you don't just
serve them well, you delight them. And we hope you're
excited about putting this system together.

I had a conversation with an academic colleague
recently who was actually my undergraduate mentor. He
said, "Jeanne, everywhere I go, customer service people are
doing tasks. They're going through the motions. They're
reading scripts. There's no ownership."

This is your chance to change that. This is your
chance to take ownership and help your team do the same,
to own your customers' outcomes and their satisfaction.

If you do that, I promise you, they'll notice.

They'll stay.

They'll buy more from you.

They'll tell other people about you.

And customers like them will flock to you.

Know this, too: We're here to help. If something isn't
clear, if you have problems or questions, or if you think you
need some coaching and facilitation to put this all in place,
let us know. You can go to www.HurlbertConsulting.com to
learn more about us or to
www.ConciergeCustomerService.com to schedule a consult.
You can also go to www.FixYourService.com to take our
complimentary assessment and get a customized report
that shows you where your opportunities lie.

References

Avanade. (2017). Executive Summary: Get Ready For the AI-first World. Retrieved from https://www.avanade.com/~/media/asset/ebook/avanade-technology-vision-exec-summary-2017.pdf

Beveridge, D. (2014). *Innovate*. Washington, DC: National Association of Wholesaler-Distributors.

Blanchard, K. and Barrett C. (2010). *Lead with LUV: A Different Way to Create Real Success.* Upper Saddle River, NJ: *Pearson Prentice Hall.*

BrightLocal. (2016). Local consumer Review Survey. Retrieved from https://www.brightlocal.com/learn/local-consumer-review-survey/

Carlson, E. (2009) 20th Century U.S. Generations. Washington, DC: Population Reference Bureau, Population Bulletin 64, no. 1. Retrieved from http://www.prb.org/pdf09/64.1generations.pdf

Chief Marketing Officer (CMO) Council and SAP. (2014). Marketers Struggle to Find Single Source of Customer Truth; Adapting to Ever-Changing Needs Key to Customer Centricity. Retrieved from https://www.cmocouncil.org/media-center/press-releases/4933

Cohn, D., & Taylor, P. (2010). Baby boomers approach 65–glumly. Washington, DC: Pew Research Center. Retrieved from http://www.pewsocialtrends.org/2010/12/20/baby-boomers-approach-65-glumly/

Colby, S. L., & Ortman, J. M. (2015). Projections of the size and composition of the US population: 2014 to 2060. *US Census Bureau*, 9.

Dimensional Research. (2013). Customer Service and Business Results: A Survey of Customer Service From Mid-Size Companies. Retrieved from www.DimensionalResearch.com

Drake, B. (2014). 6 New Findings About Millennials. Washington, DC: Pew Research Center. Retrieved from http://www.pewresearch.org/fact-tank/2014/03/07/6-new-findings-about-millennials/

Fry, R. (2016). Millennials Overtake Baby Boomers as America's Largest Generation. Washington, DC: Pew Research Center. Retrieved from http://www.pewresearch.org/fact-tank/2016/04/25/millennials-overtake-baby-boomers.

Fry, R. (2017a). Millennials Aren't Job-Hopping Any Faster than Generation X Did. Washington, DC: Pew Research Center. Retrieved from http://www.pewresearch.org/fact-tank/2017/04/19/millennials-arent-job-hopping-any-faster-than-generation-x-did/

Fry, R. (2017b). 5 Facts About Millennial Households. Washington, DC: Pew Research Center. Retrieved from http://www.pewresearch.org/fact-tank/2017/09/06/5-facts-about-millennial-households/.

Goffee, R & Jones, G. (2013). Creating the Best Workplace on Earth. *Harvard Business Review.* Retrieved from https://hbr.org/2013/05/creating-the-best-workplace-on-earth

Harter, J. K., Schmidt, F. L., & Hayes, T. L. (2002). Business-Unit-Level Relationship Between Employee Satisfaction, Employee Engagement, and Business Outcomes: A Meta-Analysis. *Journal of Applied Psychology,* 87, 268-279.

Harter, J., & Agrawal, S. (2014). Many baby boomers reluctant to retire. *Gallup, January,* 20. Retrieved from http://news.gallup.com/poll/166952/baby-boomers-reluctant-retire.aspx

Healthcare Research Institute. (2013). Harvard Scoring Healthcare: Navigating Customer Experience Ratings. *Price Waterhouse Cooper.* Retrieved from http://assets.fiercemarkets.net/public/webinars/pwc/april2013/console_slides.pdf

Hogan, H., Perez, D., & Bell, W. R. (2008). Who (Really) are the first baby boomers. In *Statistical meetings proceedings, social statistics section; Alexandria, VA.*

Hurlbert, J. S. (1991). Social Networks, Social Circles, and Job Satisfaction. *Work and Occupations,* 18, 415-430.

Keckley, P. and Coughlin, S. (2012). Survey of U.S. Health Care Consumers: The Performance of the Health Care System and Health Care Reform. United States: The Deloitte Center for Health Solutions. Retrieved from https://www2.deloitte.com/content/dam/Deloitte/us/Docum ents/life-sciences-health-care/us-lshc-2012-survey-of-us-consumers-health-care.pdf

Luca, M. (2016) Reviews, reputation, and revenue: The case of Yelp.com. *Harvard Business School NOM Unit Working Paper*. Retrieved from https://papers.ssrn.com/sol3/papers.cfm?abstract_id=1928 601.

Mendoza, M. L. & Maldonado, C. O. (2014). Meta-Analytic of the Relationship Between Employee Job Satisfaction and Customer Satisfaction. *Suma de Negocios,* 5, 4-9.

Merton, R. K. (1995). The Thomas Theorem and The Matthew Effect. *Social Forces*, 74(2), 379-422.

Patten, E. and Fry, R. (2015). How Millennials Today Compare with Their Grandparents 50 Years Ago. Washington, DC: Pew Research Center. Retrieved from http://www.pewresearch.org/fact-tank/2015/03/19/how-millennials-compare-with-their-grandparents#!14

Pew Research Center. (2017a). Internet/Broadband Fact Sheet. Washington, DC. http://www.pewinternet.org/fact-sheet/internet-broadband/

Pew Research Center. (2017b). Social Media Fact Sheet. Washington, DC. Retrieved from http://www.pewinternet.org/fact-sheet/social-media/

Pruchno, R. (2012). Not your mother's old age: Baby Boomers at age 65. *The Gerontologist*, 52(2), 149-152.

Reilly, R. (2013). Engagement Makes All the Difference. *Employment Today.* Retreived from http://www.employmenttoday.co.nz/databases/modus/hrm ag/etmagazine/JRNL-179-ET-27?tid=826567&si=1878974479

Roff-Marsh, J. (2015). *The Machine: A Radical Approach to the Design of the Sales Function*. Austin, TX: *Greenleaf Book Group Press*.

Taylor, P. and Gao, G. (2014). Generation X: America's Neglected 'Middle Child.' Washington, DC: Pew Research Center. Retrieved from http://www.pewresearch.org/fact-tank/2014/06/05/generation-x-americas-neglected-middle-child/.

United States Bureau of Labor Statistics. (2017). Labor Force Statistics from the Current Population Survey. Washington, DC: United States Department of Labor. Retrieved from https://www.bls.gov/cps/cpsaat03.htm.

United States Bureau of the Census. (2006). Selected Characteristics of Boomers 42-60 Years in 2006. Retrieved from http://www.census.gov/population/age/publications/files/2006babyboomers.pdf.

Weber, Max. 1978. *Economy and Society.* Berkeley, CA: University of California Press.

www.HurlbertConsulting.com